D0891556

Positive Moves

OTHER BOOKS BY CAROLYN JANIK:

Money-Making Real Estate

All America's Real Estate Book
   (with Ruth Rejnis)

The Complete Guide to Co-ops and Condominiums
   (with David T. Goldstick)

The Woman's Guide to Selling Residential Real Estate
   Successfully

Selling Your Home

The House Hunt Game

Positive Moves

THE COMPLETE GUIDE TO MOVING YOU AND YOUR FAMILY ACROSS TOWN OR ACROSS THE NATION

Carolyn Janik

Weidenfeld & Nicolson
New York

Copyright © 1988 by Carolyn Janik

All rights reserved. No reproduction of this book in whole
or in part or in any form may be made without written
authorization of the copyright owner.

Published by Weidenfeld & Nicolson, New York
A Division of Wheatland Corporation
841 Broadway
New York, New York 10003-4793

Published in Canada by General Publishing Company, Ltd.

Library of Congress Cataloging-in-Publication Data

Janik, Carolyn.
   Positive moves : the complete guide to moving you and your family
across town or across the nation / Carolyn Janik. — 1st ed.
      p.   cm.
   ISBN 1-555-84102-3
   1. Employees, Relocation of.   2. Moving, Household.   3. Relocation
(Housing)   I. Title.
   HF5549.5.R47J36   1988   88-4107
   648'.9—dc19   CIP

Manufactured in the United States of America

Designed by Irving Perkins Associates

First Edition

10   9   8   7   6   5   4   3   2   1

Contents

PART III   Things to Do

Introduction

To the Relocating American:

Some of the events that change our lives are marked and noted. We celebrate a graduation and we anticipate and prepare for the birth of a baby. Other events just happen. You lose your job. Or you inherit a business three states away. Or the boss calls you into his office and makes you an offer you can't refuse. Quite suddenly, you can find yourself traveling a new road in an unfamiliar environment. Your life will be changed as you become one of the 17 percent of Americans who move during each year. Feelings of personal loss will be inevitable and times of stress will be unavoidable. Neither, however, should be unmanageable.

"Hold it right there!" you and a hundred other readers cry out. "Moving is tough. Talk about loss . . . It's damn hard to leave good friends, family, and familiar places behind. And stress? Hasn't anyone told you that selling and buying a home is right up there in the top twenty on the human anxiety list? Add to that the thought of packing up everything you own, pulling the kids out of school, finding new doctors, plumbers, car mechanics, baby-sitters, etc.,

etc.! How can you sit there complacently and write 'Neither, however, should be unmanageable' and expect anyone to take you seriously?"

Because it's true. Literally millions of people go through the experience of relocating every year and just about everyone survives. In fact, many people do rather well.

Relocation does bring on the pain of separation from all that is familiar. It does mean facing countless demands as you work to find your way and your place in a new community. But it also provides abundant opportunities for personal growth and financial betterment.

Yes, I am saying that you can come through your move happier and richer. But there's an *if* that qualifies that rosy picture. A relocation means making choices. *If* you choose carefully and act wisely, moving can be a plus in your life.

I can hear your next objection already, and I agree. *Choose carefully* and *act wisely* are much easier to write than they are to do. In fact, large corporations, the government, and the military have all recognized the risk factors and problems inherent in transferring an employee, and all have been developing and redeveloping programs to make the experience easier. If you are involved in an employer-generated transfer, therefore, you will almost certainly get plenty of help in making your choices, along with considerable financial support. But no matter how good the help, no employer's relocation program can or should be a yellow brick road to be followed without question.

That's where this book comes into the picture. In it, you'll find questions to ask your employer in order to get all the benefits you can get. You'll also find answers to other questions that you may have asked already without getting satisfactory replies.

If you're moving without the support of an employer, don't despair. The force of an IBM or an Exxon is certainly an advantage we'd all like to have behind us, but it's not an essential element in successful relocation. You, acting as an individual, can save (and even make) megabucks buying and selling your real estate and moving your household goods. You can also get most of the relocation advice that is provided to transferees (at considerable cost to their employers) while spending little or no money of your own. It's a matter of knowing where to look and what to look for. Both of which I'll tell you.

The process of successful relocation, however, involves more than just packing up furniture and swapping real estate. Most people who move want a place to call *home*, and home is more than the house or apartment in which one lives. Home is a feeling, a sense of belonging, rather than a possession.

Nowhere in this book or in any other book is there a guaranteed ten-step program to feeling at home. And no amount of money can buy a home. Each person must *create* one. This creative process, like all others, requires time, effort, and perseverance.

The work of making your living place into your home can be made easier, however, by that same *if* of choosing carefully and acting wisely. For example, you'll certainly feel at home more quickly if you choose to live in a community and a style of housing that is well suited to your personality and your lifestyle. This book will offer you suggestions on how to do just that, and it will include specific, workable techniques to help you build a sense of belonging in your new community.

And then there's the question of money. Because financial stability and security are major factors in feeling at home, this book will pay considerable attention to state-of-the-art techniques for saving and/or making money as you relocate.

To fulfill all these promises without writing an encyclopedia and without drowning you in a hailstorm of bits and pieces of advice, I faced the job of finding a way to separate and organize the many tangible and intangible aspects of relocation. After filling several office wastebaskets with crumpled sheets of paper, I came up with three categories, "Money," "Feelings," and "Things to Do," and divided the book into those three parts. Each part is organized to help you anticipate and manage potential problems and stresses within its field of focus.

In the real world of *your* relocation, however, money, feelings, and things to do will not be separated into three neat and tidy sections. Each concern will be woven into and through the daily life of each person involved in your move. Mixing and melding will be inevitable. Conflict and confusion are likely to show up, too. At times, you and each member of your family will be called upon to recognize, sort out, and deal with events and emotions that may have come cascading down just like the carefully stacked stuff you tried to move from the top shelf of your closet. This book is intended to help you to pick up and reorganize your particular moving jumbles until the day comes when you look back upon your relocation and call it a *positive move*.

Oh, and one more thing . . . the element of luck. It will certainly play a part in the success of your relocation. I wish you the very best of it!

CAROLYN JANIK
Basking Ridge, New Jersey

PART I

Money

CHAPTER 1

Company Offers

OUR NEIGHBORS, two houses down the street, moved to Belgium last month. They'll be there on company assignment for four years, living in a suburb just outside Brussels. Am I jealous? You bet I am! Their relocation is the kind of company offer that prompts people to say, "No! That can't be!" But it is.

During the years that Richard works in Brussels, he will receive a generous cost-of-living increment in his paychecks. Not a raise, mind you, just extra money each month because it costs more to rent a house outside Brussels than to make the monthly mortgage payments he had been making on his house here in the States. It doesn't matter that Richard and Susan bought that house ten years ago, when interest rates and prices were a good deal lower. They get the cost-of-living increment anyway.

"Okay," you say. "He got a good deal on take-home pay. But what about that house in the States? If he sells it, he's going to have to pay taxes on all the profit he's made since the day he and his wife bought their first house. And when they come back, they probably won't have enough money to buy anything like the house they're selling, especially the way houses are appreciating in the Northeast.

Maybe the romantic idea of living in Europe makes *you* jealous, but not me. Your neighbors are getting transferred right out of the U.S. real estate market!"

Not at all. Richard and Susan are not selling. They're going to collect that cost-of-living allowance in Belgium while their house down the street from me goes right on appreciating. They've rented it, and even though the rent is almost double their mortgage payment, their company is paying all the costs of professional rental management.

And that's not all. All of their furniture and belongings that were not shipped to Belgium at company expense will be stored in a climate-controlled warehouse until they return, also at company expense. Their teenage son will attend a private, bilingual high school in Brussels, on the company. And, two days ago, Susan's Old English sheepdog was flown to Brussels on TWA.

The dog may have traveled cargo-class, but Richard, Susan, and their son are relocating first-class all the way. The company has absorbed all of the "Money" and most of the "Things to Do" worries of the move. In the "Feelings" category, it has representatives in Brussels who are trained to assist the family in adjusting to a new culture and in making social connections. The only problem this transferred family faced was saying good-bye. And that's something no corporation can do for anyone.

The Growth of Relocation Perks

Of course, if you are, or are about to become, a corporate transferee, you're not nearly as concerned with what Richard and Susan got as you are with what you'll get. Each employer has its own relocation policies. To some extent, the benefits you receive will depend not only upon the company policy, but also upon how well you read the relocation manual (if there is one) and upon what questions you ask of whom.

Company relocation programs have evolved in response to the

needs of employees, the goals of employers, and, in some cases, the reluctance or downright refusal of employees to do what the company wanted. Back in 1982, for example, the Employee Relocation Council, a Washington-based trade group, polled five hundred U.S. firms asking what was the number-one roadblock to executive relocation. The answer was no surprise at a time when mortgage interest rates were lapping at the high watermark of recent history: *real estate*. Fears about buying and selling a home in an uncertain marketplace and outrage at the prospect of paying 18 percent interest for a mortgage loan had brought employee refusal to accept a transfer to a point that was seriously affecting corporate management strength.

The business world reacted to this profit-jeopardizing situation with innovative, generous, even daring programs, some of which had never before been tried. Several corporations made special arrangements with Wall Street investment firms to offer transferees home mortgages at rates well below the current market. AT&T employees, for example, were being offered 12 percent mortgages when 17 percent was the going interest rate at most lending institutions in the area. But even 12 percent was considerably higher than the 8 percent or so that most prospective transferees were paying on the houses they currently owned, so mortgage differential payments became a common feature of many relocation programs. Some companies also instituted programs to guarantee against any financial loss to the transferee from the sale of his or her home. Others offered generous cost-of-living pay increases rather than, or in addition to, the temporary mortgage payment assistance. And some employers even offered "gross-ups," which are cash payments to the employee to cover the additional federal or state income taxes he or she might have to pay due to taxation of the relocation benefits offered by the company.

These attempts to deal with employee resistance to transfer in the early eighties have helped to shape the employer-sponsored relocation process as we know it today. Most of the programs that were initiated by leader corporations between 1981 and 1985 have not only been retained by those corporations but have also been assimilated into the relocation programs of many other employers, including the federal government and, more recently, even the military.

As the end of the decade approaches, however, companies are again meeting with employee resistance to transfer, and real estate is again among the most frequently mentioned reasons. This time, however, there is a slightly different twist. In the past four years, the Northeast and California have become economic hot spots. High-paying jobs seem to have opened up like the blossoms on a cherry tree. Because of the draw of these jobs, housing shortages have developed and home prices and rents have skyrocketed.

Few employees from other parts of the country now want to move into these high-priced areas because such a move will mean a step, or perhaps several steps, down in housing space and style. Newly structured cost-of-living pay increases or perhaps some other, more creative, incentives are almost certain to be added to relocation programs in order to stimulate transfer acceptance.

Another reason for transfer refusal that is being heard more and more often these days is "my spouse's job." Two-career couples are fast becoming the norm in this country, and in many instances the incomes are close to equal. Few professionally employed spouses want to give up their careers to follow their mate's transfer, and even fewer couples can afford the loss of the spouse's income. Some companies are addressing this issue with spouse relocation and employment assistance programs. In fact, spouse relocation is becoming a major issue and an important perk in many relocation programs.

And, finally, there is an intangible. Beneath the noise of rock music and the glitz of fast-track advertising, there seems to be a growing conservative movement in this country. Many Americans are reevaluating the importance of roots, family, community spirit, and quality of life, and some are choosing these values above the enticement of more money. What will this do to corporate and government attempts to put the best person into the job in New York City, or in Podunk? That remains to be seen.

Your Particular Perks

Will *you* get all the new benefits as they are added to relocation packages? Probably not. Various employers will try out various incentives until it becomes apparent that some work better than others. Word of success gets around quickly, and the relocation perks that stimulate transfer acceptance and best satisfy employees will probably be assimilated into the programs of many companies over a period of time.

I'm sure I don't need to tell you that it's important to keep in touch with changes in your employer's policies. Do *not* assume that things are just about the same as they were when you came to Happyville on a transfer three years ago. But there's also a step beyond that. If being transferred is a regular part of your life, try also to keep abreast of what is being offered by employers in fields entirely different from yours.

Articles on relocation appear frequently in financial-advice and business publications and in major newspapers. Of course, you can't read every issue of every business publication in the nation, but there's an easy way to keep up with news on a specific topic of interest. Just go to your local library. The reference librarian there will help you to use the library's indexes to get lists of everything published on moving or relocation during the past year or two. Read through the titles in the lists and choose those that you think might contain information on employee relocation programs. The library staff will pull the publications you choose from their files. In an hour or so, you'll be as close to up-to-the-minute as you can get without an intelligence network within the Fortune 500 companies.

But speaking of an intelligence network, you may actually have one that you don't even know about. If you live in an area where there are a number of different industries, you may have sources among your friends and acquaintances. Information on employee relocation programs can be, and often is, exchanged over dinner at a local restaurant, on the third tee, in the locker room at the tennis club, waiting to pick up the children at the day-care center, or during the monthly Cub Scout pack meeting.

To give you a frame of reference upon which to base your questions and your research, I'll take you on a tour of today's relocation marketplace by supplying you with a list of questions that will pretty much cover the range of benefits being offered by various employers across the nation. As you read through it, however, bear in mind that there is no universal standard. Your company's benefits package may be better or worse, more or less extensive, than that offered by another company located in the same industrial park where you work.

Make a list of the benefits to which you are entitled. I mean a written list, on paper, not mental notes! Check everything twice, keeping in mind that your benefits may be different not only from those of your neighbor who works for XYZ Company but also from those of your friend Tom who works in the same company as you do but in a different division and at a different rank.

"Hey! That's not fair!" you might be tempted to say.

Probably not. But no one said life had to be fair. If you wish to protect your professional status in your company, you won't go about crying "UNFAIR PRACTICES!" in the hallways. And you won't make categorical demands of your supervisor just because you have discovered that privilege increases with status. (It almost always does.)

Instead, use the program offered to you to its fullest advantage while being aware that there are other programs and benefits being implemented in your company and others. With this awareness, you are more likely to have the savvy (and perhaps the courage) to ask for a special concession if your particular relocation creates a special problem or need in your life. You might well be surprised to discover more flexibility in your employer's program than you thought possible.

No, I'm not merely fantasizing hopefully. According to a survey of the 606 companies selected from *Fortune* magazine's top U.S. companies and conducted by Merrill Lynch Relocation Management, Inc., 67 percent of the participating companies made exceptions in their relocation program guidelines to accommodate individual transferees' special needs in 1986.

If your employer has a written relocation program, be aware also that no such document has ever won an award for literary excellence. Sentences—indeed, sometimes even whole paragraphs— may be ambiguous or difficult to understand. Ask for clarifications and for the specific details that pertain to your particular problems. Knowing both the privileges and the limitations of your employer's program *before* you act can prevent painful and costly errors.

With these points in mind, read through the following questions, checking each against your company's relocation program. And don't worry if these questions give rise to new questions in your mind. The focal point of each question will be explained in more detail in its appropriate chapter. If you can't wait to find an answer, however, you can check the index at the back of this book. There you'll be referred to the pages where a given topic is discussed.

ABOUT TRANSPORTATION OF HOUSEHOLD GOODS

· Exactly what expenses will your company pay? Will they pay to have the movers pack and unpack your goods and furniture? If you must do your own packing, will the company pay for crates and boxes?

· Can you choose your moving company or will your employer make the choice?

· Will your goods be insured? Insurance is available by the pound, at the current value of the goods, and at full replacement value. Which of these options will your company pay?

· Will your company pay the extra for you to have exclusive use of the van?

· Will your company pay for storage of your household goods if your new residence is not ready for occupancy when the van arrives?

- Will your company pay the extra fee for a guaranteed delivery date for your goods?

- Will your company pay for the transportation of pets? By air? Are there any limits on size? Kind? Will they pay, for example, to transport a horse from Connecticut to California?

- Will your company pay for shipment of your second car? How about both cars? Motorbikes? Your teenager's all-terrain vehicle or your snowmobile? How about your boat?

- Will your company pay for long-term storage of selected items when your assignment is for a specified time and you intend to return to your current home?

ABOUT ASSISTANCE IN THE SALE OF YOUR HOME

- Will your company pay real estate commissions?

- Will your company (or their third-party designate) actually buy your home from you? How is the price to be determined? Or will the company advance you your equity and take over the management of and the payments on your property until a sale is consummated?

- How many appraisals will be used in determining the value of your property? If the fair market value estimates of two appraisers are not within reasonable relationship to one another, will another appraiser be called in? What other methods might be used to determine value?

- Will your company pay you a bonus if you sell your property yourself or through a broker but without using the company purchase plan and the third-party management company? How will that bonus be determined? A flat amount, a percentage of the selling price, or a percentage of the appraised value?

- Will your company allow for capital improvements protection? If you just put a $5,000 roof on your house (which, of course, does not increase its value by $5,000 since people expect a good roof), will your company reimburse you for all or part of the cost of the roof? If you put that roof on eighteen months ago, will they still help to pay for it? A part of it? Are there item limitations on capital improvement assistance? Few companies, for example, will support the cost of a swimming pool.

· Does your company offer unexpected profit protection? For example, if the third-party company should sell your property for more than its appraised value (which means more than they paid you for it), who will get the extra profit? Some company plans specify that such profit will go to the transferred employee.

· If you are selling a condominium apartment, will your company pay monthly maintenance fees between the time you move out and the time the property is sold and closed?

· If you are selling a co-op apartment, is your company willing to submit to the board of directors approval of new buyers? (This can take from a few weeks to months, and buyers can be turned down legally for any reason not prohibited by civil rights legislation. This leaves a lot of reasons for rejection!) Will your company pay the co-op maintenance fee in the interim? Will they pay the flip tax if there is one?

· If you are a tenant, will your company pay any fees associated with breaking your lease? Will your company help to find a sublet tenant and take over rent collection and forwarding to the landlord?

ABOUT ASSISTANCE IN FINDING A HOME

· Does your company use a relocation counseling service (either in-house or under contract) that is independent of any real estate brokerage business?

· Will your company pay your expenses during house-hunting trips? How many trips? How many days each? Usually, expenses are paid for husband and wife, but you might ask if the children may be brought along on one of the close-to-making-a-decision trips. And how about a long-standing companion or a relative, other than your spouse, with whom you share your home and who will move with you? Will his or her expenses be covered on house-hunting trips?

- Will your company pay for assistance in finding an apartment to rent? Will they pay the real estate agent's or rental agent's fee? Will they put up the security deposit that is required?

ABOUT ASSISTANCE IN PURCHASE

- Does your company provide for a home inspection by professionals?

- Does your company choose the home inspection service or do you choose it? Is radon gas testing included? A termite or other pest inspection?

- Does your company provide you with access to its own attorneys to review your purchase contract? If not, will they pay for this service from an attorney of your choosing?

- Exactly how many of the closing costs will the company pay? Among the most common are: lawyer's fees or closing company's fees, title search, title insurance, mortgage application fee, mortgage insurance up-front fee, mortgage points, survey fees, transfer taxes, recording fees, appraisal fees, credit report fees, lender's inspection fees (usually for new construction only), and notary fees.

- If high interest rates will mean higher monthly mortgage payments, will your company assist with mortgage differential payments to you? For how long? Are special company-backed mortgages available? At better than market rates? Are shared appreciation mortgages available in return for extra down payment money?

- If your company is not buying your old home outright, will they lend you, without interest charge, the amount of equity you have in that house so that you can close on the property you want to buy? (This is almost as good as buying your old house as long as the company assumes responsibility for the care and sale of that house.)

- Will your company arrange to maintain your old property and make all necessary payments (mortgage, taxes, maintenance fees, insurance, etc.) until it is sold and closed? Check through your homeowner's insurance policy. In some areas, premiums go up incredibly when a house is vacant. Will your company pay the higher rate?

· Does your company offer tax gross-ups to cover the cost of the higher federal and state income taxes you will have to pay as a result of factoring in your relocation benefits?

· Does your company offer a decorating allowance? (Called "curtain money" in the trade.) Is this a fixed amount or a percentage of the purchase price of your new home?

· If the property you are buying is not ready for occupancy upon your arrival in your new town, will your company pay your living expenses in a hotel or temporary apartment? For how long?

· If the transferred employee goes on ahead to the new town while the remainder of the family stays behind to sell the property or finish out the school year, will the company pay for living quarters for the employee? For how long?

ABOUT SPOUSE RELOCATION

· If your spouse is employed outside the home, will your company make efforts to find her or him a job within its own departments? And not just a job, but a job that will be commensurate with her or his skills and training? If such work is unavailable within your company, will they use networking systems with other employers in the new area to help your spouse find such employment?

· Will your company assist in résumé preparation and pay the fees of a professional employment agency in finding a position for your spouse?

· Is relocation counseling and/or therapy available for the employee, spouse, and family members if it is needed? Will your company pay all or only part of the fee for such therapy? For how long?

CHAPTER 2

On Your Own

I HAVE OTHER FRIENDS not as fortunate as Richard and Susan. In fact, theirs is a story that almost answers the question: How bad can it be?

Several years ago, Monty lost his job when the top New York City publicity firm where he worked was bought up in a corporate takeover. But, at the time, he and his wife, Ann, were not worried. They honestly believed that they could get along on Ann's salary as a city social worker until Monty found another job.

After several months with no success, however, money was getting tight. It was then that the job offer came in from Holiday Inns in Memphis. It seemed almost too good to be true. The salary was higher than Monty had hoped for, and the company even offered to pay Monty's moving expenses. The couple bought a beautiful, brand-new house in the suburban area just outside Memphis.

Sounds pretty good so far, right? The boom came down eighteen months later. Holiday Inns announced a management cutback and last hired was first fired.

My friends found themselves unemployed in a city where housing was not appreciating and jobs were not plentiful. (Ann had had to give up her career in order to accompany her husband to Memphis and had not yet found another position.)

I'll spare you the details of how they lived on temp work income and skip to Monty's next job offer. Ironically enough, it was back in New York City. But no perks this time. No moving expenses, no interim living expenses, and definitely no help in the real estate marketplace. Monty and Ann were on their own.

It took almost a year to sell the house in Memphis. During that year, they lived apart. Ann took what temp jobs she could get and tried to keep the house in showplace condition. Monty lived in a one-room apartment in New York City. They both sighed with relief when a buyer for the Memphis house finally materialized.

But their story doesn't end at that point. Where to live became an overwhelming issue in their marriage. City or suburb? And if suburb, which suburb? In which state? New York, Connecticut, and New Jersey all offered both positives and negatives.

Among the myriad of questions that became issues were where to live while house-hunting, where to store their furniture, and where to deposit the cash from the sale of their house in order to facilitate getting the best possible mortgage when the time came. Meanwhile, they paid per-week rates in a hotel and spent a fortune on kenneling their two dogs.

Monty and Ann's marriage survived their two relocations, but just barely. It was a time of many-faceted and seemingly unrelenting stress. After the financial pressure of supporting two living spaces was dissipated by the sale of the house in Memphis, there seemed to be a constant need to make decisions. And each decision they made seemed to give birth to a half dozen new decisions to be made, each demanding attention. Never was there enough time or enough information.

No Cushions

Two factors differentiate a personally motivated relocation from a company-sponsored one: money and information. Moving on your own will cost you money. In contrast, your neighbor, who is being transferred by his employer, will often *make* money on his move.

If you own real estate, moving on your own will also involve risking money, lots of it. And the risk factors are not always manageable. When all the dust of your relocation has settled, you can bet that luck will have played a role in the state of your bank account. There are ways, however, to stack the financial odds in your favor. I'll go through most of them with you in this chapter and expand further throughout the rest of this "Money" section.

It's What You Know

Before we get into the dollar signs, however, let's talk about information. Lack of it makes moving tougher for the millions of people who relocate without company support each year. If you rent, can you break your lease without financial loss? Can you make money by subletting? Is the money you might make worth the risk?

If you own real estate, how do you find out what your home is worth? How can you evaluate the communities around your new job location? How do you determine home values in each community? How do you find a good house inspection firm or a good lawyer in a state you've never before visited? How do you find temporary housing if your permanent housing isn't ready when you arrive?

These are but a few of the many questions that confront people on the move. And questions like these always seem to come up when a person has but little time to seek out the answers. As a result, relocating men and women often experience a kind of panic, which almost as often results in an "I'll take anything I can get" attitude. It's no wonder that many people who move on their own can be heard swearing from among the half-opened boxes that they'll never do it again.

What are these people missing? Well, employees on a company-supported move are almost always interviewed about their needs and interests. The information they provide is fed into a computer and lists of appropriate neighborhoods and housing styles are speedily printed. The employee and his or her family are usually shown videotapes covering not only the housing available in the area but also the schools, recreation facilities, municipal services, even the restaurants. Once they have made some selections about the probable towns, neighborhoods, and housing styles in which they would like to live, these employees are directed to real estate agents that have demonstrated their ability to handle relocation effectively. And transferees are given lists. Lists of reliable home inspection firms, appraisers, lawyers, movers, furniture rental agencies, pet transportation services, temporary housing agents; lists of just about anything relating to housing and resettling.

"That's very nice," you say. "But when you're moving on your own, you have neither the time nor the money to hunt down all these services. You have to go with the best you can get within your budget and within the time you have available."

Wrong! Oh, so wrong. You *can't afford* to "take what you can get," especially when both your money and happiness are at stake. And what's more, all of the information provided to the transferee is either free or available at little cost to you.

Private relocation services are springing up around the country. Many of these companies do not charge for their services since they receive referral and advertising fees from other service companies. Others charge the independent relocating client from $100 to $400. The range in price reflects both the variables in the services requested and offered and the differences in going rates from one part of the country to another. If you must pay for your relocation counseling, think of the fee as an investment that can save you thousands of dollars and months, perhaps even years, of unhappiness resulting from a decision made without adequate information.

For the names and addresses of relocation assistance companies located near the area to which you are moving, you can call the Independent Relocation Consultants Association at (800)

235-5585. Or you can consult the Employee Relocation Council directory mentioned on page 19.

There are also real estate brokers across the country that are opening relocation counseling offices separate from their sales offices. These brokers assign a salaried employee, one not working to make a commission by selling you property, to assist you with your relocation. Such counselors will do a family preference profile and an affordability profile, show you videotapes of areas and housing that you both can afford and will probably like, and then load you down with written information about the towns, schools, recreational opportunities, banks, service clubs, shopping centers, and just about everything you can think to ask about.

Once you choose a community and housing style, and if you're satisfied with the relocation counseling that you have received, the counselor will usually choose an agent for you from among the company's sales staff. Care is invariably taken that this salesperson's personality and style will harmonize with yours, and the matches are usually quite successful. But, remember, you have no obligation to stay with the agent chosen for you. If you are dissatisfied, you may either ask for another agent within the company or go to another real estate office in the area.

If you can't find an independent relocation counseling service or a real estate firm with a separate counseling office in the area where you are moving, you can usually use any relatively large and responsible real estate sales office to get much of the same information. Just ignore the sales pressure you're almost certain to get when working with an agent who is paid by commission.

Besides relocation counseling offices and real estate brokers, virtually all of the major moving companies have gotten into the relocation advice-giving business. For the cost of a stamp or a phone call, you can get a variety of printed matter including such treasures as area maps, cost-of-living profiles, local magazines, slick guides on what to do before you move and how to adjust to a community once you get there, and even slicker guides to local services, banks, professionals, schools, etc. And, of course, each packet sent to you will contain a full-color brochure on how Cloud 9 Movers serves you best.

"Really?" you say, wanting very much to believe me. But you're not quite sure. "How do I find these real estate firms that have special counseling offices? Or the firms that work regularly with company-supported transferees and have all the special support materials available? Or the moving companies with the most experience and support services in long-distance relocation? In other words, how can I get the company-sponsored services free?"

It's so easy you probably won't believe what you're about to read. There's a directory.

The Employee Relocation Council (ERC) is a membership organization of corporations that regularly transfer employees and relocation service companies involved in employee transfer. Every year in February, ERC publishes an oversized paperback book (it's about the size and shape of the Manhattan Yellow Pages) for the use of their members. It lists real estate appraisers, brokers, and relocation service companies across the nation who work with company transferees. The volume on my desk right now has 1,360 pages and includes state-by-state market maps that show the approximate population of each town and city, lists of real estate brokers and the corporate clients they have served, and relocation service companies such as area and relocation consultants, cost-of-living consultants, furniture rental companies, home inspection companies, household goods transportation services, mortgage services, pet transportation services, temporary housing agencies, and more.

The good news is that anyone can order this directory. As of this writing, it costs $20 prepaid. If you're interested (and you should be if you're moving on your own), you can call the Employee Relocation Council at (202) 857-0857 and ask about the ERC directory. If you prefer to write, their address is: Employee Relocation Council, 1720 N Street, N.W., Washington, D.C., 20036. Remember, however, that you must enclose payment with your order.

If you order this directory, you will have available exactly the same information that is being used by the largest and wealthiest employers across the nation. And you'll be on your way to being a well-informed relocating American. So let's go back to money and work through the list of looming expenses.

Moving Costs

People on company moves do little or no work. The moving men pack everything right down to the salt and pepper shakers. (They even packed the rock collection that my five-year-old son had hidden under his bed!) They load the van, transport the goods, unload the van, place the furniture, unpack the boxes, and take away the empty cartons and packing materials. It's carefree and expensive. You can, however, buy exactly this total-care service when you move on your own. Or you can buy any of a number of variations and you can shop for bargains.

Before the deregulation of the moving industry in 1980, it didn't much matter which company you chose for your interstate move because rates were set by law. Today, long-distance moving is an open ball game only loosely controlled by government regulation. Moving within a state is regulated by each state individually and regulations vary, so check with your state transportation office for current information on your state's laws. And be aware that there are renegade movers in every state who have not registered with the proper agency. They will work at dirt-cheap rates, and they may or may not drive off into the sunset with all your belongings.

Even the method of pricing an interstate move has changed. Before the eighties, you got an estimate of cost, but there was no assurance that the estimate would have any particular relationship to the bill that was presented to you when the van arrived at your new location. That price would have been determined by the weight of the goods in the fully loaded truck. You can still use this estimate and actual-weight procedure, but there is another option available.

Today, you can actually get a binding bid on your move. Public relations people in the moving industry will usually tell you that a binding bid will be higher than a nonbinding estimate in order to protect the carrier. They say that you will probably pay less in the end if you take a chance on the nonbinding estimate. This may or may not be true. What is certain, however, is inflexibility. If you choose a binding bid, you cannot add anything to the list of items you intend to transport without incurring the considerable paperwork of doing a *new* binding bid.

If you are moving within your state and only a short distance, you can and probably will pay for your move on a per hour basis. Rates vary across the country. No matter what rate you are quoted, however, be sure to discuss exactly what the fee covers with the company's representative. Get the agreement in writing.

In today's household goods transportation marketplace, you can also pay extra to guarantee your pickup and delivery dates. If the van fails to arrive on the specified date, the moving company will pay you a penalty fee. Currently, these payments are usually set in the $100-to-$125-a-day range plus living expenses for you and your family. This is a big-enough penalty to speed things up in all but the most impossible situations.

Another improvement since deregulation is an expanding spectrum of insurance options. But let me save insurance for a little later in this chapter and go on with money concerns right now.

Since deregulation, the transportation of household goods has become a more competitive business. Statistics show that consumer complaints are down and that there are a number of special promotions and discount deals available from time to time. Moving companies in search of business have been known to make 10 or 15 percent discount offers if you move off-season (usually October through March inclusive). Or you might be able to negotiate a discount on packing boxes or special crates for mirrors and paintings. One major mover recently offered its customers free one-way airline tickets to their new destination.

Even with the temptation of discount specials, however, it's still a good idea to get at least three estimates from major movers before you decide upon your carrier. Be sure that you give the same information to each company, specifically the distance to be traveled and which goods are to be transported.

But how do you choose the best three movers to call in for estimates? You can't possibly know what the major moving companies are offering until you talk with them, and you certainly don't want to listen to the sales pitches of every single major mover who has a representative in your area.

If yours is an interstate move, try calling the corporate headquarters of each of the national interstate moving companies and ask about rates and special offers. Almost all of these companies are now offering some assistance or incentive packages for people moving without company support.

If yours is a move within your state, you can still call the national companies and ask for the names of representatives in your area and about discount programs. You should also check your Yellow Pages, however, and make some phone calls to the independent firms listed there. You may find that a small, local mover will give you a better price on a short-distance move. Be sure, however, that the firm is reputable. Ask for references. Yes, I mean the names and phone numbers of people they have moved in the recent past.

If you want more information on moving procedures and the names and phone numbers of major moving companies, you can also write or call one of the two major national trade groups: Household Goods Carriers' Bureau, 1611 Duke Street, Alexandria, VA, 22314, (703) 683-7410; or American Movers Conference, 2200 Mill Road, Alexandria, VA, 22314, (703) 838-1930.

By calling the corporate headquarters of all the major carriers, you'll have up-to-the-minute information on incentive programs and offers, and you'll know what relocation services each is offering. With this information in hand, you can choose which three or more local representatives of national carriers you wish to invite into your home for estimates. The decision from that point depends upon what you hear from each representative.

For those on a particularly tight budget, there's also the do-it-yourself method. Rent a truck or a trailer. If you choose this option, however, the work of moving will become a major factor in your life and you'll soon find out that there's more to the move than packing, loading, driving, and unloading. Before those activities, you must select a truck rental company. There are both bargains and rip-offs in this industry. For example, some companies give lower off-season rates. Now, that doesn't sound unusual, I know, but you may be surprised to hear that there are also lower rates based on destination, origination point, and direction being traveled.

As I write this, it costs less to rent a U-Haul truck from California to Dallas than it does to rent the same truck from Dallas to California. Why? The U-Haul Corporation says they need trucks in Dallas. So call around and talk with sales representatives before you make a decision. Again, it's good to do this at the national headquarters level. Unbelievable as it may seem, some local agents are unaware of special offers being made by their own company. Take my word for it, the money and time you spend on the phone will be well rewarded.

When comparing prices among truck rental companies, ask for details. The following are ten questions you should have answered from each company.

1. Is there a drop-off charge?
2. What's the cost of insurance on the truck—liability and collision. (You may be covered by your own car insurance policy. Check with your insurance agent before you sign any agreement with the truck rental company.)
3. Can you rent dollies, pads, and other moving aids and at what cost?
4. Is the rental fee quoted you based upon a given number of miles and days allowed for the move? What if it takes longer?
5. Will the truck rental company guarantee the price it quotes to you? (Some do-it-yourselfers have been taken aback by sudden price increases that "went into effect just yesterday.")

6. Will the truck rental company assist you in estimating the size of the vehicle you will need? This is very important, since a mistake (too small a truck) can cost you megabucks, not to mention time!

7. Are there printed materials available that will assist you in the correct packing and loading procedures for maximum safety?

8. Can you hire men through the truck rental company to assist with packing and loading at one or both ends of the trip? At what cost per man-hour? Are the workers bonded? Who pays if workers drop your china cabinet and the glass is shattered and the wood gouged?

9. Is cargo insurance available? What does it cost? What will it cover if your goods are damaged in an accident on the trip? (Some truck rental companies recommend that the customer take out a rider on their homeowner's policy rather than use the rental company's insurance policies. Check with your insurance agent to see what is best for you.)

10. How are repairs to the vehicle handled in case of breakdown? (If you are unfortunate enough to get an old truck that breaks down on a highway in Wyoming on a Sunday evening and all repairs must be handled through the company's St. Louis office, you could become very unhappy.)

Finally, there's the question of what you're going to pack your treasures in. Of course, you can go to the grocery store and ask for empty soup or dog-food boxes. These work pretty well for most things and they're free. If you want to get fancier or you need special cartons, you can buy them from most carriers. You can even arrange to have special crates built for your computer, that clock you inherited, or the Tiffany mirror you bought at an estate auction.

Insurance

Major moving companies offer various kinds of insurance on your goods, each kind at a different rate. Goods can be insured by weight. (You'll never get even a fraction of their value back if the trailer disconnects from the cab and falls over a cliff!) Goods can also be insured at current value. (The television set you bought five years ago isn't worth half its purchase price today.) Or goods can be insured at full replacement value. (The company will give you the money to buy a comparable new television set if yours is crushed by the piano.) Discuss with each of the local moving company representatives what these various plans cost. You might also check with your homeowner's insurance company or read through your policy to see if your goods are already insured while in transit and to what degree.

If You Rent Your Living Space

If you are currently renting and intend to continue renting, your money risks are small. If you break your lease (leave before it expires), you'll probably lose your security deposit and, in some cases, you may be asked to pay a default fee. But don't just assume this will happen and leave in the dark of the night. Have a talk with your landlord. He or she may just give you all or part of the deposit money back, especially if vacancy rates are low in the area and you give enough notice to allow the landlord to arrange for a new tenant to move in soon after you move out. Of course, it goes without saying that you must also have left the apartment undamaged.

On the other hand, few landlords are willing to go to court to force you to make rent payments to the end of the lease's term while the apartment stands vacant. They usually just rent to someone else.

If for some reason you do encounter legal difficulties over the lease, you might consider a sublet. In a tight rental market, you might even charge more for your sublet than you currently pay each month. But choose your replacement tenant carefully, for you are still responsible under all the terms of the lease including rent payments and damages. And be sure to read your lease carefully before you consider a sublet. Some leases specifically prohibit subletting without consent of the landlord.

Finding an apartment in your new location can be a breeze or a blizzard. It all depends upon the housing situation in the place you are moving to. If you have the ERC directory, call some real estate agents in the area and ask about vacancy rates. If the vacancy rate is above 5 percent, you should have little problem finding an acceptable place to live. Anything under 5 percent, however, may require a good deal of footwork on your part.

"Well, I'll just have an agent take me around," you say.

Don't you wish! In suburban areas, some agents will spend a day or so showing you rental houses and the few apartments in the multiple listing books. But rental commissions are small and you really can't blame the agents for wanting to spend the time with a potential buyer. There are, however, rental specialty agents in most larger cities.

If you don't want to wait until you get to your new city before contacting a rental agent, you can get phone books for the major cities in the United States at your local library. If the library doesn't have the actual books (they take up a lot of shelf space), they will probably have microfilm files available to you. The friendly people at the desk will show you how to use the microfilm reading machine. Some of these machines will make copies of the material on the screen with the push of a button, so you can take copies of whole telephone book pages home with you. When you make your calls, bear in mind that most real estate agents who specialize in rentals work in an area close to their own offices. It's a good idea, therefore, to have a map of your destination city available and plot your calls so that you contact agents in different areas.

If you can get Sunday newspapers from the area you will be moving to, you will see advertisements for both new and vacant apartments. Call for more information if you are interested. In large apartment buildings or garden-type complexes, there is usually a rental agent on the premises and there is rarely a commission.

If you use a real estate agent for your apartment-hunting, you should find out who will pay the agent's commission. In some areas, it is the seller, but in many areas, the buyer must pay all or part of the fee. If you don't want to get stuck owing money you didn't plan for, ask about local and office practices from each agent you deal with. Or, better yet, ask who pays the commission for each apartment that interests you even slightly. Commission is usually one month's rent, and this extra money might influence your decision, especially if you intend to stay in a given apartment only a short while.

If you wish to rent in a multifamily house or in a small apartment building, you will have to go door-to-door. Most of these property owners do their own tenant selection, and, of course, there is no rental commission. Your best source of leads for these apartments will probably be the classified section of the local newspaper. But don't discount word of mouth as an excellent source. Talk with people. Tell them you are apartment-hunting. A co-worker or a hotel employee might just give you a lead on a lovely place to live. In some large corporations, there is also a housing list on which local people can advertise their rental units. Ask if your company has such a list.

Buying and Selling Your Home

This topic is so complex and its opportunities for making or losing money are so numerous that it will take most of the remainder of the "Money" section of this book to discuss it adequately both for you and for the corporate transferee. The process is actually similar for you both in most aspects, except risk. Essentially, risk is minimal for the corporate employee, whereas avoiding risk is a prime concern of the person moving without employer support.

The question most often asked by homeowners who are moving without company assistance is: Should we buy before we sell, or sell before we buy? And I'm afraid there is no right answer. But let's look at some of the known advantages and disadvantages.

If you sell before you buy, you will know exactly how much money you will have to spend on your next home and you will know when you will have that money. These are advantages that vaporize a good deal of anxiety, but that mental ease comes with a disadvantage. Once your house is sold, you usually must move out quite soon. This means getting a place to live as soon as possible in the new location. Under these circumstances, you will have to choose from what is available in a given week or you will have to arrange temporary housing and plan to move twice. The double move and the probable storage of some of your household goods may cost you considerable money.

If you decide to buy before you have sold, you can house-hunt without pressure while your old house is on the market and you can snap up a property that has particular appeal or one that is an especially good buy whenever you see it. The chief disadvantage of buying before your old house is sold is financial. You may be required to close on your new house before you close on your old. If you need the equity you have built up in your property to do this, you will probably have to get a bridge loan (usually at a relatively high interest rate) and you will have to continue making mortgage, property tax, and insurance payments on your old house as well as taking on these same payments for your new home.

So what should you do? Much depends on your financial situation and the moods of the real estate marketplace in the area you are leaving and in the area you are going to.

If you have plenty of extra cash, you might as well choose your new house while your old house is up for sale. Sign the contract to buy whenever you find exactly what you want. You can, of course, ask that your closing date on the house you are purchasing be made contingent upon the sale of the house you are selling, but most sellers will refuse this request. It's just too iffy for them. They have no control, and theoretically you could overprice the house you are selling and force them to wait a year or more before you sell it. On the other hand, you will occasionally come upon sellers who will allow such a contingency, if you make it worth their while financially or if they themselves need time to find another house. So there's no harm in asking for this safety net.

If the sellers say no to making their sale contingent upon the sale of your old house, try to negotiate more time (three or four months) before the closing date on your new house. This will give you extra time to sell your old property and save double carrying costs and perhaps even bridge loan costs.

If the market is very hot in the area to which you are moving, you may feel pressured to buy whatever you can. Or you may decide to rent until you find the place you want. You have two years after you sell your home to find another of equal or higher price before the IRS requires you to pay federal income taxes on the profit from the sale of your home.

If the market is also hot in the area you are leaving, you can pretty much count on a quick sale, and buying before you sell may be of little risk. To gauge the temper of the market in your area, ask several real estate agents about the pace of the marketplace. Ask how long most properties remain on the market. Ask how close actual selling price is to original asking price.

If your local marketplace is slow, it may be best to wait until you have a firm contract before you decide to buy. This may entail one family member moving ahead to the new job while the remainder of the family stays behind until the house gets sold. Such an arrangement is stressful, but, believe me, it is not as stressful or as expensive as carrying two houses when you can't really afford to do so.

Taxes

Normally, taxes are a terrible place to end a chapter, but tax concerns are a part of your relocation and, in some cases, a means of saving money. Both the direct and indirect expenses of moving to a new location *because of a job change* are deductible on your federal income tax return.

Direct moving expenses include the cost of moving your household goods and personal property from your old location to your new one. The costs of packing, of boxes, crates, and other packing materials, and of any in-transit storage are also deductible.

The expenses incurred while getting yourself and your family to the new location are considered direct moving expenses. They include transportation, meals, and lodging. Under the current tax law, however, only 80 percent of the cost of meals is deductible.

Indirect moving expenses are of three types: (1) the expenses of premove house-hunting trips; (2) food and lodging while waiting to move into a new home; and (3) certain expenses of buying or leasing a residence. In category three are such items as the costs of settling an unexpired lease, acquiring a new lease, real estate agent's commissions, escrow company fees, attorney's fees, appraisal fees, title costs, loan placement fees, and mortgage application fees. This list is incomplete and subject to change, however, so be sure to check on all available deductions with a tax specialist when you are ready to move.

As of this writing, there is a $3,000 overall limit on the deduction of indirect moving expenses. Furthermore, the portion of indirect moving expenses that is deductible for meals and temporary lodging cannot exceed $1,500. But here again, I am working with numbers that are subject to change with every shift of political winds.

To qualify for tax deductions for moving expenses you must satisfy two tests. *The distance test*: your new job must be at least thirty-five miles farther from your old home than your old job was from your old home. If there is no former place of work, your new job must be at least thirty-five miles from your former residence. *The thirty-nine-week test*: an employee must work full-time in the general vicinity of the new job location for thirty-nine weeks during the twelve months following the move. A self-employed taxpayer must continue work at the new location (as a self-employed person or as an employer) for at least seventy-eight weeks during the twenty-four months following the move, of which at least thirty-nine weeks must be in the first year.

Relocation-related tax deductions can save you a good deal of money or, more correctly, can get you a nice refund after you file your return. But let me repeat again that tax laws are both complex and subject to unexpected change. I urge you, therefore, to consult an up-to-the-minute tax guide (the IRS gives them out free) or a good tax adviser before you calculate your relocation tax deductions.

A Final Word

Moving on your own is not the great adventure that the do-it-yourself truck rental companies would have you believe. It's tough work, full of stress, and in some cases risky. Your best safeguards against trouble are organization and knowledge. So make plans, gather information, and ask questions!

CHAPTER 3

Getting Ready to Sell

JOHN CONNERS was ecstatic when the news of his promotion and transfer came through. So was Betty. The kids were too young to care much, one way or the other.

"Glory be! We're really going to get rid of this place," he exclaimed. "And in Savannah, we'll get twice as much house for the price we'll get here. Man! We're on a roll now!"

John and Betty focused all their energy on the information the relocation people gave them about Savannah. In fact, they just crossed their present home off their concern list. They would take the company offer, whatever it was, and not be bothered with the work of fixing it up or the intrusion of showing it to prospective buyers. As a result, they lost thousands, maybe even tens of thousands, of dollars.

When your company offers to buy your house, they usually base their offer upon the valuations gathered from one to three professional appraisers. The figures these appraisers present to your employer are their estimates of the fair market value of the property. But no one *really* knows the fair market value of a piece of real estate until a ready, willing, and able buyer makes an offer that a ready, willing, and able seller finds acceptable. The Connerses, in their excitement over their transfer, just assumed that whatever the company said would be about as much as they could get.

They forgot two factors: (1) Appraisers are people. They respond consciously and subconsciously to dirt, clutter, and disrepair just as other people do. And (2) appraisers are paid for their professional opinion as to market value. Through experience, they have learned to factor in peeling paint, missing doorknobs, shrubbery gone wild, and even dirty windows as indicators of probable selling price and time on the market. These factors may not be as important as location and square footage, but they do matter. Appraisal is not an exact science. How the appraiser evaluates your property is affected by his or her response to it.

Whether you are moving on a company transfer or moving on your own, and no matter how much you can't wait to get out and get going or how much you just don't want to go, you must take the time and make the effort to put your present home into salable condition in order to get top dollar for it. And you must do this before company appraisers or helpful real estate agents doing their competitive market analyses of your property appear at your front door. So let's take a tour around your property and I'll point out the areas and factors that most affect selling price and make a few suggestions.

Curb Appeal

You've certainly seen those before-and-after grass seed advertisements in magazines—the weed-filled, overlong, scraggly-looking *before* picture and the ready-for-the-cover-of-the-magazine *after* picture. Ideally, you'd like your appraisers, the real estate agents, and your prospective buyers to see your property only as an *after* picture. With a transfer or an independent move looming, however, perfect *after* impressions are not always possible. (It can take many weeks before the best seeding and fertilizing job in the world shows any real results.)

What to do? Here are some tips I've picked up while working as a residential real estate agent and in the course of our many moves.

The grass. Cut it often. If you keep everything short, it's hard to tell the weeds from the good stuff.

Edges. Trim them. Even a newly cut lawn can look overgrown if a bevy of weeds and long grass fringes every tree, the curb, the edge of the driveway, and the walkway to the front door.

Foundation plantings. Do a careful job of pruning. Foundation plants have a way of getting bigger over the years. Because we're so accustomed to the plants around our homes, we don't notice that the Japanese holly is blocking out 20 percent of the light from the dining room windows. Nor do we notice that the pachysandra leans out eight inches over the front walkway, since we hardly ever use the front door ourselves anyway.

Your front door. Look at it carefully. It is a point of curb focus and either a welcoming or an unwelcoming symbol. If it needs some TLC, paint it. And if there's a chance that you won't be able to match the color to the existing trim of the house, be creative and choose an entirely new color for the door. It is quite stylish right now to have an entranceway painted in an accent color.

House painting. A not uncommon notation on a Realtor's listing form is "$5,000 painting allowance," which means the seller is telling the prospective buyer to take $5,000 off the asking price before negotiation even begins. And that's just about what a new paint job is worth in the home-buying marketplace, no matter what it really costs you to get the job done. It's also just about what peeling paint will cost you in a company-sponsored appraisal.

Now, if you're leaving in two weeks, you hardly have time to paint the entire exterior of your home. But if it's really in bad shape, you should check to see what it would cost to have the job done by professionals. Then make a decision based on this cost versus probable return.

If you take a tour around your house and notice that only the trim is flaking and peeling (which is often the case), you might consider trying to do that job yourself. Often, freshly painted trim is all that's necessary to give the whole place a newer, brighter look.

The Living Area

I really have only two words of advice in this section: *clean* and *uncluttered*. But being a writer, I'll just go on with a few more bits and pieces.

When you are preparing to sell your home, try to look at each room as though you were seeing it for the first time and as though you do not live there. Look at the pictures on the walls, the furniture arrangement, the draperies, the bric-a-brac. Does it all go together? Really? Or has it more or less accumulated over the years and just been left because it isn't bothering anyone?

The foyer. If you're in the habit of storing out-of-season coats and sports equipment in the foyer closet (and who isn't?), take all that stuff out and hide it somewhere. One or two coats hanging there will give the closet a used and useful look, but your prospective buyers and your appraisers should perceive how much space is available, not how well you've filled it.

The living room and the family room. Most people want space and comfort in a living room or family room. Graciousness and good taste don't hurt either. Individuality, artiness, or exotic touches, however, don't count for any extra points and may even detract from salability. Your goal is to make these two rooms appealing. Anyone should be able to look into the room and want to spend time there.

Achieving this type of appeal may take a little work. It will certainly mean removing anything that fills space without contributing to grace and usefulness, including Aunt Martha's hope chest, your golf trophies, the four-foot-high papier-mâché cat sculpture that won first prize in the school art contest when Sylvia was in fourth grade, and the cabinet overflowing with board games the kids never play anymore. Your goal is the kind of look a designer would arrange for a magazine photo session. Lots of charm, but nothing too personal.

Most of the work in these two rooms will be focused on removing things, but you might think about adding a few plants. Generally, people find living plants appealing and they are very good camouflage for the dents in the carpet left by the furniture you removed.

Lots of how-to-sell-your-home books suggest that you build a roaring fire in the fireplace for every showing. This is nonsense. The first prospective buyer who comes in may be impressed, but the second won't like the smell of smoke and ashes in the air. And your appraisers will not be impressed, except perhaps in knowing that your fireplace works. But they will assume that anyway.

So unless you like cleaning up ashes several times a week, sweep them up once, get out your vacuum cleaner and take up the dust you can't sweep, and then go out and buy some lovely white birch logs to stack in the grate. A basket of eucalyptus branches on the hearth adds an appealing odor to the air.

The kitchen. The heart of the house, as they say. Kitchens sell more properties and wreck more deals than any other room. Look at yours as though money depends on it. It does.

Take everything off the counters, even if this means getting the toaster out every morning and putting it back into the cabinet below the counter while it is still warm. Good work space (which translates as clear countertops) earns many plus points.

Next, look at your windows and curtains. Most people like sunny kitchens. Get those windows sparkling clean, replace the curtains if they are frayed and limp, and be sure not to block out the sun.

Speaking of bright and sunny, look up at your ceiling. Kitchen ceilings have a way of getting gray and spotted. You may be able to detect signs of smoke from the occasionally burned toast, grease carried up from the oven vent, and maybe even a few spots from the bottle of sparkling burgundy that just wouldn't open until Uncle George took it into the kitchen to work on it. Consider a paint job.

No one will ever thank you for it; in fact, most people will not notice, but your kitchen will look brighter and more pleasant for your work.

Bathrooms. Clean! Clean! Clean! Consider a new shower curtain and throw rugs. (You can take them with you.) Get the grime out from between every tile (floor and walls). Sinks, tubs, and toilets should shine, literally. And if the caulking around the tub has turned black in spots, recaulk or buy a set of ceramic tiles specially designed for edging tubs. (Available at most tile stores.)

Bedrooms. Take as much as you can out of the closets. A good place to store these extra things is under the bed. No one ever looks there. Get your kids to take down the three-foot-by-four-foot Twisted Sister poster that is the first thing everyone sees upon entering the room. Put away all of the half-finished craft projects that you're going to get to soon. Keep the shades raised completely or the blinds fully open in the daytime to let in maximum light. Sunny is a plus in bedrooms, too.

The Garage

Here, again, you want to give the impression of maximum space. Organize your lawn and garden tools. You can hang rakes, shovels, etc., on the wall rather than pile them in a corner. Mops and brooms, too, if you store them in the garage.

Your goal is to have appraisers, real estate agents, and prospective buyers feel that the garage will handle not only the cars for which it was built but also the bikes, tools, sports equipment, skateboard runs, extra refrigerators, and all the other miscellany that we tend to store there.

The Basement

If you don't have time to run a garage sale to get rid of some of the extra stuff you've been carting along for years before the appraisers come in for their inspection, stack everything neatly. You want to leave maximum open floor space. Check that every light bulb in the basement works. Dark basements worry people. You might even replace those 60-watt bulbs with 100s. And wash the windows if there are any. I know, this is bothersome work, but you want all the light you can get.

Take your vacuum cleaner down to the basement and vacuum up the spiderwebs and dust balls wherever they have gathered. Then call your heating contractor to come out to clean your furnace. You may be thinking that this is certainly an unnecessary expense, but soot lying about the furnace will worry both buyers and appraisers. "Maybe something's wrong with the furnace," they'll think. And then they'll ask you how old it is and probably how old the water heater is, too.

Pets

Those of us who love and live with our own pets are rarely put off by other people's. But there are many, many people who object strenuously to animals actually living in the same house with human beings! Don't allow the fact that Shakespeare and Napoleon sometimes sleep on your couch to decrease the value and salability of your home.

Clean cat litter boxes more faithfully than you ever have before. Have someone take your dogs for a walk before the appraiser or prospective buyers arrive or confine all your animals to travel crates or in a pen in your backyard.

And whether your pet is a cat, a dog, six gerbils, a ferret, or a parrot, spray some *unscented* room deodorizer about before anyone drives up for a house inspection tour. ("Hawaiian Garden" hanging in the air of a Maryland tract house is worse than the scent of a litter box!)

Decorating

Just about every spring, *Practical Homeowner* magazine features a home-improvement cost/value survey. And just about every year, interior painting and decorating come up as the most value-adding home improvements you can make.

On a transfer or a time-pressured move, you may not have much time for redecorating and your intellectual and creative energies may well be directed to where you're going rather than where you are, but if you want top money for the property you will be selling, stop and take yet another look around. If woodwork is badly chipped, repaint it. You will be amazed at how much newer every room will look. If your child has crayoned the walls of his or her room, consider putting up a textured wallpaper in a neutral color. If a particular room's paint has been on the wall so long that its original yellow has turned to gold, repaint the walls *and* the ceiling. (Bright walls and a dingy ceiling make poor bedfellows.)

It's Worth the Effort

I can almost hear you thinking.

"What a bother! We have to do all this just when we're so damned busy and a little shook up too over the move itself! And we won't even get to enjoy the results of our work. Someone else will move into those newly painted rooms!"

Well, you're normal. Just about everyone feels the same way. But let money be your motivator for a bit, and try to do what you can to add value to your housing investment. If you can get it all done *before* the appraisers, real estate agents, and prospective buyers arrive, you will increase your odds for financial rewards that will certainly help to make your life a little better at your new destination.

CHAPTER 4

What's It Worth?

"GOOD MORNING, Happy Hearth Real Estate."

"Ahhhh, good morning. I, ahhhh. I was driving on Sunny Brook Road yesterday and I saw your sign on a house there. Could you tell me what the price is?"

"Certainly, Mr. Ahhhh. May I please have your name?"

Silence.

"Why do you need my name? I just want to know how much that house is."

"Of course, sir. The asking price of 29 Sunny Brook Road is $198,000. Would you like any other information? Or would you care to come in and talk about other properties that are available in the area?"

"No, thanks anyway."

Click.

While I was working as a residential sales agent, there was a standing, tongue-in-cheek rule in our office: just ignore the first five calls after the sign goes up. Anyone who had worked in residential real estate for more than a month knew that those calls would probably be from the neighbors.

"Why would the neighbors call to ask about a house for sale?" you wonder. "They already live in the neighborhood!"

Oh, they don't want to buy it. They just want to know the asking price. You see, nothing influences the value of a home as much as the value of other properties in the neighborhood. Those five or six callers that we'd get on every sign we put out really wanted to know the current value of their own houses. They'd hear the price named and then begin mental calculations. Was their house bigger or smaller? Better or not quite as nice?

This technique for determining value may sound somewhat unsophisticated to you, but in fact it's the professional appraiser's primary tool for determining the probable value of residential property.

Appraisals

If you are moving with company support that includes assistance in the sale of your home, you will probably meet at least two appraisers. If you are moving on your own, you may or may not use an appraiser, probably not. But before we get into the whys and hows, let's go through what a residential appraiser does.

The Society of Real Estate Appraisers, a national trade organization, describes a relocation appraisal as: *the probable price for which your home will sell in the current market within a reasonable length of time*. This group defines "reasonable length of time" as approximately four months, but qualifies that by saying that it depends upon prevailing market conditions.

Most real estate brokers and appraisers will tell you that an appraisal is an estimate of fair market value. To people in the trade, fair market value means the highest price that a ready, willing, and able buyer will pay and the lowest price that a ready, willing, and able seller will accept. Which brings us back to what the house will sell for in a reasonable length of time. Remember, therefore, that an appraisal is an educated *estimate*.

By far the most commonly used method of reaching this educated estimate figure is the comparative sales approach. The work usually begins in the office before you see the appraiser and before he or she sees your property.

With the address of your property in hand, the appraiser digs into the comparables files. Comparables are records of properties that have been sold in your area over the past several years. The records include a description of each property, usually with a photo, the original asking price, the actual selling price, and the length of time that it took to sell the property. After going through this information, the appraiser will have a ballpark figure for the value of your property.

"Stop right there," you say. "You mean to tell me that the appraiser has a price in mind before he or she even sees my place? That doesn't sound very professional to me."

It is. Very few residential properties sell for more than 15 percent above or below the median price for the neighborhood. Of course, there are occasional exceptions to that rule of thumb, but that's exactly why the appraiser will not only visit but also inspect your property. After studying the comparables, the appraiser has an idea of value in mind. The inspection is a fine-tuning of that idea.

Getting Ready for the Appraiser

Be prepared for the visits of your appraisers. Information that you can probably find with just a little digging about in desk drawers can, and probably will, have an effect in determining each appraiser's estimate of value. Have on hand the following:

- A copy of the professional survey of your property with the house, any other buildings, and permanent markers such as a stone wall, clearly indicated.

- A copy of the local tax map or of the plat plan for your tract development, which shows your property in relationship to the others around it.

- If your house is fairly new, a list of special features, often called extras, that were built into the house at added cost to the buyer. (This item is particularly important if new construction is still going on in your area.)

- A list of improvements that you have made since you bought the property. If possible, machine-copy documents that establish the cost of these improvements and give them to the appraiser.

- A list of personal property that is included in the sale. Personal property in the real estate industry is anything that is not attached to the house or land. It might include a washing machine, lawn furniture, draperies, carpeting, etc.

- A list of items currently attached to the house that will not be included in the sale. Most common among these are dining room chandeliers, but sellers have been known to take all curtain and drapery rods, window shades, children's swing sets, punching bags attached to the beams in the cellar, fixed fireplace screens, even installed wall-to-wall carpeting.

When the Appraisal Is Done

Accompany the appraiser during the inspection of your property. Answer all questions as accurately as you can. In an older property, you may be asked the age of the furnace, the age of the water heater, the date of the last septic tank cleaning, or a number of other facts that might help to establish the condition of working systems.

After the appraiser bids you good day and goes out the door, don't be surprised if you see him or her measuring your foundation with a giant tape measure. Square footage and replacement costs are backup figures for the appraiser's market comparison estimate.

Most companies that transfer employees with home sale support hire two appraisers to make separate evaluations. Usually, the company offer is the average of the two price figures. Most companies also have a safety net on these figures, however. If the appraisals differ by too much (the most common acceptable difference is 5 percent), a third appraisal is usually ordered. If that comes within 5 percent, or whatever the established figure is, of one of the other estimates, the average of those two figures is usually taken.

Appraisal is more difficult if your property is very unusual, very expensive, or very distant from other properties. It's hard to estimate what a houseboat, or a church that has been converted into four condominiums, is worth until the market is tested and a buyer actually appears. Sometimes even three appraisals will be very different from each other. In such a case, a specialist can be called in. Most home insurance companies employ or maintain lists of appraisers who work exclusively with unusual properties. You or your company can employ such an appraiser to evaluate your home. Of course, it costs a bit more, but it may settle an otherwise knotty problem.

Speaking of costs, the price of an appraisal differs greatly across the country, from one section of the same state to another, and even within the same town. For the transferee, this makes no difference since the appraisal is arranged and paid for by the company.

If you are moving on your own, however, and for some reason you want an appraisal, be sure to call several appraisers to compare their fees. There is no set fee. It's a competitive marketplace. Most homeowners who are about to sell, however, do not need an appraisal. You can get all the information in an appraisal without cost or obligation. So why pay? I'll tell you how to do it, but first let me spend just a bit more time with my transferee readers.

Using an Appraisal

Once you get the appraisal figures and know what the professionals think your property is worth, you have two options. You can accept the company offer, which will mean that your home will not be put up for sale until after you move out, or you can put your property on the market.

Choosing the second of these options, however, does not necessarily rule out selling to the company. Most employers allow a period of time (two months is common) for you to make a decision. During that time, you can try to sell for more than the company offer by marketing your home through local real estate agents.

There is also a new and growing trend among employers to pay transferring employees a bonus if they sell their homes through local real estate agents rather than take the company offer. These bonuses may be stated as fixed amounts (say $5,000) or as a percentage of the sale price (5 percent is common). And the bonus is paid to you in addition to the payment of the real estate commission.

"How can they afford to do that?" you ask.

Actually, the employer saves money. Independent specialty companies that handle the sale of a transferee's property are called third-party companies in the relocation trade. Their fees are high and are fixed *in addition* to the real estate commission that will be paid to the broker who actually sells the property. So when the transferee sells his home through a real estate agent, the commission is a common fee and the bonus paid to the employee is usually much less than the fee that would be paid to a third-party company.

If you are a transferee who wishes to try selling on the open market before accepting the company offer, be sure that you have a corporate rider clause written into the listing contract that you sign with the real estate broker who will market your property. This clause must state that you are allowed to accept the company offer and cancel the listing contract at any time without payment of commission. If you don't include this clause and you decide to accept the company offer, you may get into legal hassles over breaking the listing contract since most employers use third-party companies who work with their own list of real estate agents in the area.

Estimates of Value

"Isn't an appraisal an estimate of value?" you ask, knowing that I said it was at the beginning of this chapter.

Well, it is, and I haven't changed my definition. But an appraisal is an estimate of value that someone must pay to get. Which is fine if the company is doing the paying. This section, however, is primarily for people relocating without company support, and it will tell you how to get estimates of value that use exactly the same tools and techniques the appraiser uses without paying a penny for the information.

There are real estate firms across the country that are currently offering this service absolutely free. They're even sending out letters with coupons attached that read: "Just call XYZ Realty for your competitive market analysis." CMAs, that's what most real estate companies call their free estimates of market value. You should get at least three from three different companies. Five is better.

A competitive market analysis is done by a real estate salesperson, who, more than likely, is not an appraiser. It is a statement of opinion and is not binding in any way. But by getting several CMAs from different agencies, you will hone in on market value, perhaps even more closely than from an appraiser. The real estate agents, after all, are working in the marketplace. They know exactly what is happening, now!

To do a CMA, the agent will come to your home, walk through it with you, and ask you some questions. You should have copies of all the information listed under "Getting Ready for the Appraiser" on page 42 ready for each agent who does a CMA. Sometimes, the agent will bring comparables (copies of the listings that have sold recently in your area) along and do the CMA right on the spot. Usually, however, they like to go back to their offices and do some comparing. This also gives them another chance to come back to your house.

You do understand, of course, that this is a free service, but not one without a purpose. The agent doing the CMA wants your listing. And you will have to listen to a speech about the quality of the services offered by his or her agency. Don't turn off the audio while she is doing this even if you plan to go the "For sale by owner" route. You may at some point in that process change your mind and want to choose a real estate agency to market your property. If you listened during the CMAs, you will have information that can help in choosing among the brokers in your area.

When or if the agent presenting a CMA asks you to sign on the dotted line, simply say that you intend to get CMAs done by at least one or two more agencies before you decide with whom you will list. Do not sign anything!

Like the appraisals, the CMAs should cluster around a common number. If one of your three is either very high or very low, get two more. Real estate agents are very definitely human, and the CMA is a personal response as much as it is a mathematical estimate. One agent may be turned off by your rose-colored bedroom carpet, another may think it enhances value by a few thousand dollars.

If you do decide to list your property with a broker, you should list with one of the agents whose CMA fell within the clustered price group. Sometimes an agent will give you a very high estimate of value and assure you that he or she can get that much for your property even if the others can't. Don't believe it! If four out of five companies say your house is worth $150,000 and number five says $175,000, you are not likely to get the $175,000. Most agents who give such inflated estimates are trying to win the listing with inflated hopes. They get you to sign up for six months knowing that you're planning to move. Once you've signed the listing and no one shows up to see your house, you're stuck for the whole six months. There's nothing left to do but reduce the price. You're back to the figure around which the other agents clustered, but now the agent representing you is one you don't trust so much.

About Feelings

Before I leave this chapter, I need to say a few words about feelings, even though I promised to save that topic for the middle section of this book. In this case, however, the feelings I'm talking about can affect the financial return you get from the sale of your home.

Home, there's the word. *Home*, both the physical space and the concept, is laden with feelings. Memories of holiday celebrations around the dining room table, your love for the roses you planted, the notches on the door molding that show how much little Mikey has grown, even the two stains on the family room carpet that mark places where Plato had accidents when he was just a puppy.

Once you have decided to sell, you must separate your feelings and memories from the physical space in which you live. Call it "the house" or "the apartment" and don't say "We're selling our home." It is, after all, real estate, a piece of property that you now want to sell. All the special things you love about it will not affect the selling price, so don't mention them to prospective buyers. Those buyers will find their own things to love, but when they come to look at your property, they are usually seeking value and comfort.

More potential real estate deals have fallen through because people got their hearts in the way than from almost any other cause. A woman once chased me out of her house swinging a broom in the air above my head because she was insulted that the offer I brought to her was too low. Four months later she sold that house for $500 less than my offer. This actually happened, honestly! Take heed, and try to be as rational in your pricing as you can.

CHAPTER 5

For Sale by Owner

GOOD GRIEF! You're telling me that John is leaving for Omaha in six weeks to take over his uncle's hardware business, John, Jr., is sure that he'll be put back to the JV team in any other high school in the country and thinks you've ruined his life, Tommy is sick that he's going to be two thousand miles from his best friend, Susan knows there won't be a Mariner Girl Scout troop in Omaha, and even shaggy old Chaucer has figured out that something is going on, and you've decided to put your house on the market "For sale by owner!" Why?

"You can't be serious," you reply. "Money. That's your answer. The real estate commission on this house will run nearly $15,000. We really could use that money for moving expenses or for decorating and furnishing our new house. Besides, how hard can it be to sell a house? We can show people around just as well as the real estate agents we've worked with. Maybe better."

You might be right, but 90 percent of the residential properties sold in this country are sold by real estate agents. If it's so easy, why don't more people do it? And why do so many who try give up and list with a broker?

If your tilted head and raised eyebrows and the shrug of your shoulders mean you don't really know, I'll tell you. Most for-sale-by-owner properties are overpriced. Most homeowners don't market and show their properties well. Face-to-face negotiating is tough. And even when a price is finally agreed upon, most buyers and sellers stand about uncomfortably wondering what to do next. Should there be a deposit? Who holds it? What about financing? Are these buyers qualified?

All of these problems can be solved with the insider tips that I'll give you in this chapter. But there are other reasons why homeowners don't succeed in selling their own homes. Chief among them is the character of real property. Your home can't be packed up, taken to the nearest Sunday flea market, and displayed for all strolling customers to see. Each piece of real estate is unique and immovable. A prospective buyer must go to the property in order to see it and be allowed inside in order to inspect it. Most for-sale-by-owner properties therefore sell to local residents who are at least somewhat familiar with the area. Buyers moving into town from a distance almost always use the services of a real estate agent. These facts create a relatively small pond in which to fish for a buyer.

If you still want to give this limited market a try, go for it. You might save all or most of that commission money. But if you follow all the advice in this chapter and you haven't found a buyer in four weeks, choose the real estate firm you liked best in your CMA interviews and list your property. After four weeks of sell-it-yourself advertising, you have probably exhausted the local market and need the greater exposure that a multiple listing service and a good real estate firm can give you.

If you are moving with company support, there is usually no advantage in attempting to sell your home without a broker. Most employee relocation plans pay real estate commissions. And even those plans that pay a bonus if you sell the property rather than accept the company offer usually pay the bonus in addition to the commission. But do check your particular relocation program.

Who knows? You may be the one in a thousand transferees who would profit from selling without a broker.

How to Market Your Home

The first step is setting a price that will attract potential buyers and encourage offers. But asking price is not the same as the market value figure you got from the appraiser or the CMAs. Everyone wants to negotiate in the real estate marketplace. Even if you set a price at or just below market value and advertise FIRM after it, just about every potential buyer will make offers below that price. Some will even walk away from the deal because you wouldn't come down!

The question is how much negotiating space to add into your asking price. This is a fine line to walk. Too much might discourage a tentative buyer. Too little, and an aggressive buyer won't feel that he or she got a good-enough deal. The best guidelines are to be found in the market conditions of your area.

When the real estate agents are in your home doing their CMAs, ask each one how the market is doing. Are houses selling quickly? At close to asking price? Or are houses selling slowly with large differentials between asking price and actual selling price? When the agents show you the comparables, make a mental note of the differences between original asking price and actual selling price.

If the market in your area is hot and houses are selling quickly, you can list high and take a shot at making a killing, or you can list close to market value and stand firm. Don't overprice too much or for too long a time, however. Greed has killed many a potential deal. Remember you're already saving the commission.

If the market is slow, you may want to try a little advertising hype. Inflate your asking price a bit and include a line like: "Owner moving out of state. Will consider all offers!" This may bring some buyers out of the woodwork who want a bargain. You have built some of that bargain into your asking price. If the negotiating goes on and you seem close to a deal, you may even want to agree to go a bit below the figure you determined as fair market value. Remember, that figure is an estimate and you are still saving at least part of the real estate commission.

Before you put your ad in the newspapers, however, do a little preparation work. Probably the toughest part of selling your own home is getting potential buyers to come out and look at it. If they get lost on the way, most just turn around and go home. It's too much trouble, they think. So you want to make it easy for them to get to your property.

To do this, buy a street map of your town. Mark the location of your property on the map. Then find the major roads in town and a landmark or intersection on each that will be easy to recognize. Mark those places and trace the route from each of them to your property. Now, if you could hand out copies of your marked map, your task would be easy, but the odds are your prospective buyers will not have a map. You, therefore, must provide directions.

You'll want to write out a separate sheet for each route to your property. To get accurate, easy-to-follow directions, go with a companion to each of the landmarks or intersections you designated on your map and drive the route home. Make note of your odometer reading so that your directions will be accurate to the tenth of a mile. Also make note of cross streets, traffic lights, easily recognizable landmarks, anything that will make your directions foolproof.

Now make a copy of each set of directions for each of the telephone extensions in your home and devise some way to keep those directions from straying. (Nail them down if you must!) It's essential that you be able to give clear, mistake-proof directions to every interested party who responds to your advertisements.

As a safeguard, ask that your prospective buyer "go over" (you mean, repeat back) the directions again just to be sure. You're going to be surprised at how many people ask for directions without a pencil and paper handy. They think they can keep it all in their heads. But when you ask them to go through it again for you, they just can't. Be cordial. Say something like, "I know this is sort of confusing. Why don't you get a pencil and I'll go through it again for you."

Now you're ready to put the ad in the newspaper, right?

Not quite. Another major advantage that real estate brokers have over homeowners selling on their own is the listing sheet. Agents can give their customers copies of all the information that pertains to an interesting property. The customers can take this home and consider it or compare it with other properties. Most of the questions that come to mind later, like "What are the taxes?" or "How big is the master bedroom?" are answered right on the sheet.

In contrast, most potential buyers go home after seeing a for-sale-by-owner property for the first time and can't even remember if the master bedroom had one closet or two. Many don't want to call the owner back for the information for fear of seeming too interested. And before you know it, the for-sale-by-owner house is dropped from consideration.

You can keep your property from being forgotten by making a listing sheet of your own. You can format it like the comps you were shown during the CMAs or you can simply make a list. Both methods are effective. Your information sheet should include the price, address, your name and phone number, the style of the house, its age, the size of the lot, and the number of rooms. Then, in a separate column, list each room, with its exact size and any special features such as a fireplace in the living room or a whirlpool tub in the master bath. Don't forget the garage. Below the room descriptions, list the nuts and bolts of property ownership: taxes, assessment, zoning, association or maintenance fees, waste disposal system (city sewers or septic tank?), water source, electrical service, type of heating system, fuel, and any extras included in the asking price. Don't mention closing date, however, because you may want to use that in your negotiating.

Finally, you must make a sign. You want the prospective buyer driving down your street to be able to pick out your house without hunting for house numbers. The sign should be fairly large, two feet by three-and-a-half feet is a good size, and it should be placed perpendicular to the road. You'll have to letter on both sides:

FOR SALE

BY APPOINTMENT ONLY

[YOUR PHONE NUMBER]

You can buy weather-resistant, stick-on letters at your local stationery, crafts, or hardware store.

Now, finally, you're ready to put the ad in the classified section of your local newspaper. Keep this simple. You do not need to compete with real estate brokers. Most prospective home-buyers make a special effort to find the new for-sale-by-owner ads each week.

In your ad, include the town, neighborhood, or community, but not your street address. You want potential buyers to call you, not just drive by. Follow that with the style of your property (Colonial, condominium, contemporary, whatever), the number of rooms and the number of bedrooms, the size of the lot, and the price. Never advertise without the price. Studies show that many people simply don't call when the price is not included!

Precede your phone number with "Owner," but do not bother to add "Principals only." Real estate agents are going to call you anyway, so why pay for the extra words?

During the first few days after your ad hits the newspapers, your phone will probably ring circles around itself. Don't get too excited. About 75 percent of the calls will be from real estate agents who want the listing. Just say no.

When you do get calls from prospective buyers, try to control the conversation. Answer their questions and talk about your home enthusiastically, but also try to get their names early in the conversation. If the callers want to "drive by," give them directions from the sheets you have by the phone but remind them that the property will be shown by appointment only. Stick to this stubbornly. Even if Jimmy Carter comes to your door, tell him that you will gladly show him through your home if he'll make an appointment. The appointment can be for an hour later, but it must not be right then and there. This is for your own safety. Most people who will return for an appointment are legitimate house-hunters, and you can always arrange to have at least two people in your home while it is being shown. One should do the showing, the other should stay near a phone in another room.

How to Show Your Home

About the worst thing you can do is to walk from room to room saying, "This is the living room, this is the kitchen, this is the bathroom, this is the master bedroom," etc. What the room is, is usually apparent enough. Instead, point out plus features, or sales pegs, as the agents call them. You might say, for example, "We just put in the Jenn-Air last year. It converts to a barbecue grill on both sides," or "Robin has the smallest bedroom in the house, but the biggest closet."

While you're walking about with your prospective buyers, try also to ask questions. "Where are you folks living now? Do you have children? Have you been looking for a house very long?" These questions may sound like innocent small talk, but they are really gathering information that may be important to you if you get into negotiations over price.

Once you've gone through the main living area of a house, you will probably sense whether these people are interested or not. Uninterested buyers walk through very quickly. Interested buyers go much more slowly, return to look at rooms again, and look into closets and cupboards. If your prospective buyers seem interested, ask if they want to see the basement and/or the attic. If they do, they are definitely interested. And if they walk the property lines with you, you'll probably get an offer.

Negotiating

Try not to do any negotiating over the phone. Any experienced real estate agent will tell you that telephone negotiating loses more deals than it makes. If your prospective buyer calls with an offer (even a full-price offer), suggest that he or she or they come over and talk about it.

Now you want to sit around the kitchen table over coffee and talk. If the offer is low, do not take offense or show anger or resentment. Instead, tell your prospective buyers how hard you worked to determine fair market value for the property. Tell them about the CMAs and tell them the selling prices of similar properties in the area. Then make your counteroffer in conversation. For example: "Considering all this, we really couldn't accept $_____ [whatever they have offered]. But $_____ [your counteroffer] seems like a fair price."

A common response to a counteroffer is "We can't possibly afford that!" This is an open door. Jump at the opportunity in exactly the same way a good real estate agent would. Say, "Well, let's talk about it." While this sounds as though you mean talk about the price, what you really mean to talk about are the buyers' qualifications and the various financing options.

Get out pencil and paper and ask, "How much did you want to use as a down payment?" Once you have that figure, you can say, "Okay, that means you'll be carrying a mortgage of $_____ at our price. Most of the lenders in the area will allow you to spend 28 percent of your gross income on housing costs. That means to afford this house you'd have to be earning about $_____," and do the calculations.

If you can get your prospective buyer to participate in this type of qualifying conversation, you can quickly eliminate those people who really can't afford your property. You might be able to persuade others that with slightly different financing, they might be able to come very close to affording your property.

This is a good time to help your buyers to make a counteroffer by saying, "Well, it looks as though you can afford $_____. Are you willing to pay that for this house?"

Some buyers will say "Yes" then and there, and if the price you named is one you're willing to accept, you may be on your way to a deal. Other buyers will want to go home to think about it all, and you must allow them the time to do that. Too much pressure will only result in nervous buyers who often change their minds.

No matter how the negotiating session goes, however, remember to keep it on a rational plane. As soon as people get emotional, the deal begins to slip away. If you are far apart on price, cordially suggest that your buyers might want to think about it a bit more. Suggest that they call you if they want to see the property again or if they would like to talk with you further.

Safety Nets

If you and your prospective buyers reach an agreement on price, shake hands but don't accept a check for deposit monies. Because you don't have a real estate agent working for you, you will want to consult a lawyer about drawing up a binding contract. You should have someone in mind before you put your house on the market because your lawyer will take over many of the roles of the real estate agent. The lawyer will hold the deposit monies, for example. And if you request it, he or she can check on the employment of your buyers and can check to be sure that the mortgage has been applied for as specified in the contract. The lender should also notify your lawyer when the mortgage loan has been approved, since most contracts are not really binding until that contingency has been met. House inspection services, termite inspectors, and radon tests should also be reported to your lawyer when they fulfill contract contingencies.

You can also use your attorney or your accountant (real or

imaginary) as a means of letting negotiations cool down a bit or of buying thinking time. Negotiators in the commercial real estate marketplace often say, "Well, that's an interesting offer. I'll have to discuss it with my accountant [or attorney]. Let me get back to you in a day or two."

Using exactly this same technique, you can buy time to check your prospective buyers' employment, credit history, and probable qualification for a mortgage. Or you might just want to sleep on the offer. Maybe you'll come up with a creative counterproposal tomorrow.

While your property is being advertised "for sale by owner," I can almost guarantee that you will receive at least one special-situation call from a real estate agent. It'll go something like this: "Mrs. Seller, I'm Betty Krocker from Happy Home Realty and I'm calling for a very special reason. You see, I have these transferees that I'm working with. They have only two more days in town and I think your house would be perfect for them. Would you be willing to let me show it to them?"

What should you do? If the agent really does have transferees, you know they are unlikely to call because of your newspaper ad. And you certainly would like to get your house sold. But, on the other hand, this may be a creative agent looking for a way to "show" your house (maybe to her brother-in-law and his secretary) in the hopes that she can make an impression on you and persuade you to list with her. And, besides, you don't want to pay a 6 percent commission.

There is a solution. Offer Betty a one-day open listing. Tell her that if she sells the house to these transferees, you will pay a commission of 3 percent. She won't really be losing any money since she is unlikely to get more than that if the house were listed in a multiple listing system. For properties in MLS, most brokers split fifty-fifty between the listing and selling offices. If Betty Krocker of Happy Home Realty sells your home, she'll get the same 3 percent that she would get if she sold the listing of another broker on MLS.

To protect yourself in this kind of arrangement, have Betty come to your home without her customers. Have an open listing agreement ready for her to sign. It should read something like:

Date_____

With my consent, Betty Krocker of Happy Home Realty will show my property located at [your address] on [date]. In the event that a sale should be agreed upon and closed at [your price] or another mutually agreeable figure, I agree to pay a commission of 3 percent of the actual selling price to Happy Home Realty. This agreement is valid for this one day only.

_____

[Your signature]

_____

[Betty's signature or her broker's signature]

If you prefer, you may legally name a price in this open listing contract that is higher than your for-sale-by-owner price, thus compensating for commission by a higher asking price. Be absolutely certain, however, that the agreement you type or write out contains the words "In the event that a sale should be agreed upon and closed at." If you don't include the words "closed at," and the deal falls through, even though a contract was signed, the Happy Home agency could demand that you pay 3 percent commission because they brought you someone who would agree to the sale price.

You can also allow Betty to show your property on a verbal open listing. This is like a handshake agreement. You say to her on the phone, "Yes, you can show the house. If you sell it and we close the deal, we'll pay you 3 percent of the sales price." Most brokers will not allow their salespeople to work on open listings. But sometimes the situation is so hot that exceptions are made.

The problem is that it's very hard to substantiate the agreement when nothing is written. If Betty should sell your property on her one-day showing, be sure that the terms of commission payment are spelled out in the contract of sale. It's not a bad idea to talk with your attorney about it either.

CHAPTER 6

If You List with a Broker

WHERE DO YOU GO? What do you do while a stranger is showing two other strangers through your home? These are questions almost no one asks. Out loud, that is. But just about everyone thinks about them. And the answers home-sellers come up with are as varied as the homes in which they live.

There's the huddle approach. The entire family sits on the couch in the living room throughout the showing. They each smile and take turns holding the dog. Everyone says "Bye" as the real estate agent and customers leave, but no one gets up off the couch.

Then there's the exit approach. The owner opens the door, welcomes the agent and customers, and takes the agent's business card. "Make yourself at home," he says and the whole family goes cheerfully into the backyard, even if it's the middle of November.

Some home-sellers, on the other hand, just act as though the real estate intruders are not real. I opened a closed door one day and was astonished to find myself in a bathroom with a woman sitting in the tub. She was quite discreetly covered with bubbles, but I babbled something in red-faced embarrassment and wished my (male) customer was not standing directly behind me! The woman neither smiled nor nodded but went right on rubbing a washcloth over her arm. The husband of this woman was in another room, so intent upon shooting alien beings with his computer that he never even grunted in reply to our greeting. Needless to say, we let ourselves out as we had come in, through the front door, which no one had answered when we rang the bell.

Then, of course, there's the ever-popular vacate-the-premises option. As the real estate agent drives toward the house, she sees a woman walking from the driveway pushing a baby carriage and holding a German shepherd dog on a leash. This is unremarkable except that it's raining.

If you've ever looked at houses with a real estate agent, you can probably add a few more creative tactics to this short list. And, actually, almost any method of response to house-showings is acceptable except one: *Do not follow the agent and customers about from room to room making comments and "helping" with the sale.*

When a real estate sales agent shows your property, let the agent do the selling. Nothing puts customers off as much as a hovering homeowner. It may seem to you that the agent isn't saying enough, but, remember, a lot of talking goes on in the car and in the office. If you are asked a question, answer as clearly and completely as you can. But don't orchestrate the tour. These particular buyers may not want to see your darkroom in the basement. To insist that they follow you downstairs is a waste of everyone's time. Instead, you can guarantee that every customer will be aware that there *is* a darkroom in the basement by putting that information in your listing.

What's a Listing?

Listing has several meanings in the real estate marketplace. A listing is the sheet of paper the real estate agent shows you with the photo of the property and all the details pertinent to the sale neatly printed out. This same agent, however, will refer to a property that is for sale as a listing. He or she might say, "I have a listing on Garden Street and one on Maple Avenue." Another agent might say to you, "I am primarily a listing agent." She means an agent who takes listings. In this case, listing means the contract by which a seller hires a real estate broker to act as his agent.

Then there's the Multiple Listing Service (MLS), which is the method Realtors use to share their listings with other members of their particular trade organization. Putting a property into MLS allows competing real estate firms to show and sell the property you listed with the agent of your choice. Some sellers are put off by this sharing. They say they don't want strangers trekking through their homes.

Sometimes, in response to this objection or because of prevailing custom in a given area, a representative of the listing broker is present every time the property is shown. In most cases, however, the key box method is used. A key box looks like an overgrown padlock. Its front panel is obviously removable and has a star-shaped keyhole in its center. When the loop of the padlock is hung over your front doorknob, the key box can only be removed by someone who can open its front panel. Every sales agent in the local MLS group has a special key that will accomplish just that. Inside the key box is the key to your front door or whatever door you wish customers to enter through.

Some sellers worry about allowing such open access to their homes. And, of course, a reasonable amount of caution is justifiable. When your home is on the market, it's certainly a good idea to remove small valuables from the tops of dressers and put away your Steuben vases. But in the vast majority of cases, the key box method works, and instances of theft or damage are rare. A key box and a spot in the local MLS books will give your home maximum exposure. Sales agents will find it easy to bring customers to and through your home. And, believe me, making work easy for the sales agents will better your odds for a quick sale.

Before a real estate agent can sell your house, however, you must list it. And to list it, you must hire a real estate broker to act as your agent. There are several types of listing contracts in use in the United States. Let me run through them for you and tell you how to use each, what to watch for, and what to watch *out* for.

EXCLUSIVE RIGHT TO SELL

This is the listing contract most favored and most often used by real estate brokers. In many areas, it is the only contract that will get your house into the MLS files. It gives the broker with whom you sign the contract the exclusive right to sell your property during the term of the listing contract. Even you, the owner, cannot sell it without paying the broker a commission. By arrangement, however, other members of a multiple listing service can sell the property. Legally, they act in the capacity of subagents of your broker and they split the commission according to a prearranged agreement.

EXCLUSIVE AGENCY

This contract gives your broker the exclusive right to act as your agent in the sale of your property but reserves for yourself the right to sell the property to a buyer that you procure through your own means. (A tip through the office grapevine, for example.) Your broker may or may not choose to share this listing with other brokers in the area. Some multiple listing services will accept exclusive agency listings, others will not.

OPEN LISTING

An open listing states that you agree to pay the broker who sells your property a commission, but also that you reserve the right to sell the property yourself or to sell it through another broker. Open listings are not shared among brokers. You must sign individual contracts with each office that you will allow to show your property. Most agencies will not advertise open listings.

UNWRITTEN OPEN LISTING

If you tell an agent over the phone that it's okay to show your condo and that, yes, you'll pay a 6 percent commission if he or she sells it for $200,000, you have given that agent a verbal open listing. Such unwritten agreements often lead to the county courthouse and litigation. Get your agreements in writing.

NET LISTING

If you say to a broker, "I want $150,000 for this property. Whatever you get above that you can keep," you have given the agency a net listing. If the firm sells your property for $200,000, they keep $50,000. Now, such an arrangement might be an incentive for intensive sales work, except that net listings are now illegal in most states. And when they were legal, they usually didn't work well. Greed became too dominant a motivator.

Before you sign any listing agreement, be sure it contains the following elements:

- *The date.* A contract without a date will not hold up in court, if you should ever end up there.
- *The address of the property for sale.* Also include any other identification that is pertinent: the apartment number, for example, or the block and lot number on the town's tax map.
- *The price at which the property is offered for sale.* You may and probably will change this figure during negotiations, but you need a real number on the listing contract.
- *The name of the real estate broker or firm that will act as your agent.* Remember that most of the people you see in your home will be salespersons. A licensed real estate salesperson acts on behalf of and under the supervision of a licensed broker. The broker's signature must appear on your listing contract.
- *An expiration date.* Be certain that a specific date appears on your contract. You do not want a generalization such as "three months."

Why? Think about this: you sign a listing contract on September 30 for three months. On December 31, your brother-in-law's second cousin tells you he'd like to buy the house. You come to an agreement at a figure lower than you had hoped, but, what the hell, you don't have to pay commission! Or do you?

· *An escape clause if you're a transferee who might just accept the company offer.* Such a clause is usually called a corporate rider. It states that you may accept your company's offer to purchase your house at any time without obligation to pay a real estate commission to your listing broker.

· *The amount of the commission.* There are prevailing customs throughout the United States, but there is no law anywhere that sets the commission between a broker and a seller. You may state the commission as a percentage of the sale price or as a flat fee. The percentage method is much more widely used.

· *A statement that the commission is to be paid upon closing.* This is a protective clause for you. If a broker brings you a buyer who ties up your property for six weeks and then skips town the day before the closing, you should not owe the broker a commission.

· *A list of items included in the sale.* Don't be too generous. Extras can be used during negotiating.

· *A list of items excluded from the sale.* Be sure to list here anything that is currently attached to the house that you plan to remove. Chandeliers and drapery rods are common items. If they are attached to the property, the law says they go with the house unless you specify otherwise.

· *Signatures of all the owners of the property and the real estate broker.*

Generally, the exclusive right-to-sell contract will get your listing on MLS and be the highway to the sale. If you want to try a back road and conditions are right, however, you might choose to work with open listings. This is a method by which some savvy homeowners occasionally save thousands of dollars.

The open listing method works best in a sellers' market when properties are in high demand, there is a minimal inventory in the

MLS, and actual selling prices are coming in close to asking prices. If such a market exists when you are ready to sell your property, advertise your home "for sale by owner." Follow all the advice in Chapter 5 including the information sheet. Then call all the local real estate brokers and invite them to come to your home for an open listing. Give each a tour and a copy of your information sheet and sign a three-month open listing agreement that will be automatically terminated if you or any other broker sells the property. Most real estate firms have open listing agreement forms in their offices. If you are having trouble getting these, however, you can ask your attorney to draw up a simple, one-page form for you and machine-copy as many as you need.

But how does the open listing save you money? It's quite simple, really. When a broker enters a property into the MLS, it becomes probable that another broker will sell it. In this case, the listing broker gets half of the commission. (In most areas, residential commission is, by custom, 6 percent of the sale price. The listing broker therefore gets 3 percent if the MLS agreement is fifty-fifty.) If you give an open listing to every office in your area at 3 percent commission, those agents will be working for exactly the same amount of money they would be getting if they sold a property listed by another agent on the MLS. If you really want to stimulate sales, offer 4 percent commission. You are still saving thousands of dollars and the agents are now working for a little extra bonus. The result is usually that your property gets shown a bit more often. Most agents who agree to work under this arrangement, however, will ask that you do not put a FOR SALE BY OWNER sign in front of your property.

Choosing Your Listing Broker

You will want your property to be marketed by a firm that is local, reputable, and familiar with the type of real estate that you are selling. If you are buying a house forty miles from your current home, do not list with the broker who sold you that house unless he or she has an office in the area of your home (a five-mile radius is usually good). Even if you have been delighted with the service you received from the agent who sold you your new home and that agent tells you that her office belongs to the same MLS that lists properties in your area, you will be doing yourself a disservice by listing with an out-of-area broker. Real estate is still a local business. It is virtually impossible to adequately service a listing far removed from the office.

Also avoid the Johnny-come-lately firm that offers to take your listing for 2 percent less than the going rate. When you hire a broker to sell your home, you want a good reputation in the community and a good track record. If you think these things don't matter much when a discount is being offered you, imagine the cash value of your home *in cash* on your kitchen table. Would you allow a fast-talking, TV-real-estate-seminar–type salesperson to pack up that money and hold it for you?

Beware also of the salesperson who promises that he or she can get you $10,000 more than anyone else. This is rarely true. The technique is as old as bait-and-switch: promise them $10,000 or $20,000 more, then three weeks after they list for a six-month term, when not a single soul has been around to look at the property, suggest that they lower the price.

If you live in a condo, don't hire a farm specialist to sell your property. And don't hire your insurance agent, who also just happens to have a real estate license. And don't hire your Aunt Mary's friend who is an appraiser but belongs to the local MLS. The same advice applies if you live in a house in Levittown, a co-op apartment, a multifamily house, or the apartment above your shoe store. You want the real estate agency that handles your property to be familiar with—no, to be experts in—the sale of the kind of property that you are selling.

When You Get an Offer

If it's at full asking price and there are no contingencies to the sale (like getting a mortgage), your property is sold. Sign and do your war whoops after the agent is out the door.

But, as I'm sure you know, this rarely happens. Most real estate transactions include a nail-biting stage called negotiating. Let me give you a few tips to make it easier.

- Don't lose your temper.

- Don't let your heart rule your head. (You may love your home, but this is a business deal.)

- Don't take numbers personally. (If you were the buyer, you'd try to get all you could for your money, too!)

- Never say never.

- Allow some time between negotiating sessions.

- If the first offer is extremely low, knock off a token amount ($500 or even $1,000) from your asking price and make it your counteroffer. This is a far more satisfactory way to say, "Your offer is much too low" than simply saying "No" to the agent. A simple no confuses the buyers. They don't know if you want to play the game or not. A tiny reduction says, "We'll play, but we're going to play tough."

- If you are *approaching* what seems to be an acceptable figure to you but your buyers refuse to go any higher, try sweetening the pot with a few extras. Draperies, carpeting, lawn furniture, a riding mower, the pool table in the basement, and the playhouse in the backyard that your children have outgrown are all good negotiating tools.

- Play your cards close to your chest. Do *not* tell the real estate agent what you hope to get for the house. If you do, there's just about zero chance that you'll get a penny more. Also, *never* reveal your rock-bottom figure, unless that's what you really want for the house. Once you tell the agent what you really want, believe me, that's what you'll get. You should make every counteroffer with a straight face and no apologies.

When Is It Really Sold?

Most contracts for the purchase of real estate have a mortgage contingency. Today, many also have home inspection contingencies, termite contingencies, radon contingencies, and even drainage and well-water purity contingencies. In a real estate contract, a contingency is a stipulation that must be satisfied before the contract becomes binding. All of the above are common, but each should have a cut-off date by which the work must be completed or the contingency is waived. Your property is not really sold until all the contingencies in the contract have been met or waived.

In some states, a contract is also nonbinding during a stipulated legal review period. This is usually a short time (three to five working days) during which either the buyer or seller may consult with an attorney and either alter or cancel a contract. If this protection is not a part of the real estate law of your state, you can have it written into your contract. Of course, many people buy and sell houses without ever seeing a lawyer. But when you're dealing with hundreds of thousands of dollars, it seems to me a good idea to pay out a double-digit figure to get the contract reviewed. If you are moving on a company transfer, the legal review may be free (done by company attorneys).

As a seller, you may also choose to have a clause written into the contract that will release all the deposit monies to you once the contingencies have been met. A few buyers will object and want the money held until closing, but negotiate for its release. You can use it as the deposit on your next purchase, thus saving interest payments on borrowed money.

Above all else, be wary of any clause that will make the sale of your property contingent upon the sale of the buyers' property.

Such a clause could hold up your sale for months while the buyers try for top dollar for their property.

Also be wary of the buyers' mortgage lender. Some lenders are now writing contingencies into their mortgage commitments that require the buyers' property to be sold before they can get the mortgage money to buy another house. Do not accept such an arrangement.

When you think your house is sold, don't sit back and relax. Keep in touch with the selling real estate agent. Be sure that the inspections are being done. Ask for the results of each. And have the real estate agent follow through on the buyers' mortgage application. When was the application made? Was it made for the amount specified in the contract? If not, why not? Who is the lender? Have your agent call the lender and ask if their mortgages are ever made contingent upon the sale of the buyers' property. If that is the case, insist that the buyers use another lender. Get your attorney into the act if you must.

CHAPTER 7

Choosing Your Next Hometown

THE NEWEST INNOVATION in high-tech relocation assistance is the computerized match-up service. It's a little like a singles find-a-date company. You fill out a questionnaire, the information is fed into a computer, and, beep-beep, buzz-buzz, the printer produces several sheets describing the area communities (or neighborhoods in a very large city) where you would certainly be happy to live.

If you have or expect to have children, and if schools are high on your list of important factors in choosing your future homesite, there are also match-up services that will choose your prospective municipalities based upon how well the school system matches your educational goals and priorities. The largest of these is a service called SchoolMatch, run by Public Priority Systems, Inc., Blendonview Office Park, 5027 Pine Creek Drive, Westerville, Ohio 43801. For a fee of $97.50 as of this writing, you can fill out a twenty-two-question form and have print-outs of suggested schools for any area of the country mailed to you within twenty-four hours after the questionnaire is received.

Many corporations offer SchoolMatch as a part of their relocation packages, and transferees have been quoted in national magazines and major metropolitan newspapers as finding the service "indispensable."

You can hardly argue with the opinion that information on class size, spending per pupil, athletic programs, and mean scores on standardized tests is helpful in judging the character of a school system. But don't let the dazzle of a computer print-out blind you into thinking that the machine has all the answers. Choosing a school system, like choosing a community, has human variables involved that no machine can measure. What's the attitude toward discipline in the high school? How are leadership and community responsibility developed in the elementary grades? Is there a foreign language program in the middle school? The answers to such questions must be asked of people in positions of responsibility and observed by watching with your own eyes during a visit to the school in question.

But I'm getting ahead of myself. Let's go back and look at how you can use the skills and advanced technology of the relocation industry to help you choose potentially acceptable destinations. Then I'll add a few tips of my own on choosing a place as right for you as possible, a place that will feel like home sooner rather than later.

Using Relocation Services

Seventeen years ago, when I followed along on my husband's first corporate move, relocation assistance meant paying the real estate commission on the house we were selling and paying our moving costs. Joe got a few suggestions on "nice" places to live and the names of a few real estate agents from his co-workers, but there was no company-sponsored orientation to the area. We were flying by the seat of our pants. Quite by luck, we made a rather good landing.

Today, even the least-experienced individual or family moving independently of company support has more information readily available than we did. The relocation service industry is among the fastest-growing in the United States. There are giant third-party companies with names like Travelers and Merrill Lynch that are hired by employers to buy a transferee's home and cushion every aspect of the move, from choosing a town to financing the new living space. There are relocation services like Nationwide (a part of the Sears network) that specialize in counseling and are openly associated with large real estate firms. There are large real estate firms that have separate relocation counseling centers. Most of the major moving firms offer relocation information, some even have their own counseling centers. Even the chambers of commerce of some major cities are setting up relocation counseling centers. (New York City offers private counseling, group seminars, guided tours of New York neighborhoods, an assortment of pamphlets, and even videos.) Banks are offering "Welcome" kits with maps and area information. And virtually every real estate agent in the residential business has a cabinet full of community information giveaways.

Even before you leave your current home, you can use services such as those offered by Nationwide and a number of other firms to get cost-of-living statistics for the area to which you will be moving. When you go out on your first visit to the new area, you can sit in an agent's or counselor's office and watch videotapes that will introduce you to the character of various neighboring communities. You can ask computers for information about mean salaries, mean house sale prices, cultural and athletic facilities, and sometimes even the number of Chinese restaurants in a town. After just one scouting day in your new area, you can sit down to dinner in your hotel dining room with a list of four or five communities where the computer says you will probably find satisfactory housing.

But how can you be sure that the lists will be accurate? You want to be happy in your new home, and, if you are buying property, you want it to be a good investment. In at least a small way, the success of your housing hunt is going to affect the rest of your life. Scary, isn't it?

The Secret of Success

If you want to tap the information in real estate computers most effectively, it is essential that you put top-quality information *into* the machines. The same holds true in working with relocation service representatives and real estate agents. Give them accurate and comprehensive information about your needs, your goals, your resources, and your personal preferences.

"What's the best way to do that?" you ask.

The key words that will unlock the answer to your question were spoken when the English language was about as young (relatively speaking) as Pascal or Basic is today: *KNOW THYSELF.*

Before you begin your housing hunt, even before you talk with a relocation counselor, take some time to look at yourself and into yourself. On page 81, you will find a ratings list that I have composed to help you get started. Don't limit yourself to these items, however. Add others as you think of them or as they apply to your specific life situation. Have each member of your family who is moving with you do a separate evaluation. If you have children in your family, help them to talk about their feelings and then fill in the ratings list as you think it applies to them, perhaps even adding some particularly child-oriented items such as the number of parks and playgrounds in a community or the presence and accessibility of a municipal swimming pool.

If you want a composite family picture of your preferences and priorities, take all the premove ratings lists and make a family graph. Using a different color ink for each person, superimpose the line graphs of all family members on one sheet of paper.

When you've finished this little exercise, you will have a family profile that will be an invaluable tool in choosing where you will live and later the kind of housing you will live in. It will also contribute mightily to keeping your housing selection on a rational level. For example, it will keep you from falling in love with gingham curtains in a sunny kitchen window that may prompt you to buy a farmhouse when a condominium would have better served your lifestyle and personal preferences. It will also help you to think twice before you commit the maximum amount of your income to housing payments if you like to ski, take occasional trips to the Caribbean, or eat at good restaurants at least once a week.

Take your family profile with you when you talk with relocation service people and real estate agents. It will help these human counselors to help you. Also use its information to ask computers for the statistics you need to begin the narrowing-down process that precedes choosing a new hometown.

Printed Matter

While the computer, relocation specialist, and/or real estate agent are using your profiles to select your prospective living sites, do a little searching on your own. Housing is often a good indicator of the socioeconomic character of a community. And there is an excellent overview of housing for each of the local communities in the real estate agent's office. I'm referring to the multiple listing books.

Ask your agent to allow you to look through the books. Resist the temptation to turn immediately to your price range, however. Instead, look at the kinds of properties available in each town and make comparisons. Notice which towns have the widest range between the least expensive and the most expensive listings and note in which price range there are the largest number of houses for sale. You will see that some towns are more or less homogeneous, with the majority of housing units listed within a rather narrow range of prices. Other towns will have a wide price range, but a clustering or bulge in a certain economic group. Some towns will be mostly condominiums, others may be mostly mini-estates. Ask yourself where you see the most listings that appeal to you. Scribble some notes on what you think the multiple listing book is indicating about each of the area communities.

Take your notes, the computer's suggestions, and all the printed matter the relocation counselor can give you home (or back to the hotel) with you and study them. You will undoubtedly come up with three or four communities or neighborhoods that seem right for you. But don't carve your decision in stone.

Rate your prospective communities without disqualifying any unless you have very good and specific reasons. What you are working with so far is printed matter. It is created by the information available to, and the questions and focus of, the person who wrote or programmed it. But there's something else important in choosing a community.

For just a moment, think about judging a person. If you carefully and accurately note sex, height, weight, color of hair, eyes, and skin, critical measurements (such as chest, waist, and ankle), dental work, vision with and without glasses, and the density of bone, you will have put together a lot of information and you will have found out nothing about the potential of this person for love and friendship. It's pretty much the same with communities. They have personalities just like people, and all the statistics in the world won't replace a few hours spent together.

On a separate sheet of paper for each community that interests you even slightly, list what you see as its strengths and weaknesses and write out any questions about it that come to mind. Then spend some time in each one. Driving around is acceptable for a beginning, but walking is far superior. Go into the library of each community under consideration. Talk with the people at the desk and ask to see a few issues of the local newspaper if there is one.

Stop for coffee or lunch in a local restaurant (not a franchise hamburger heaven). Note the foods and the prices on the menu (there's a lot of information there between the lines) and talk with the person who waits on your table. Go to a local shopping area or to a small shopping mall. What kinds of stores do you find? What is being featured in the windows?

If you are fortunate enough to have a weekend available to you and you get some nice weather, go for a walk through several residential neighborhoods. Talk with people working on their lawns or walking their dogs—anyone, in fact, who'll talk back—and don't forget the children. People love to talk about their neighborhoods and their towns. And every conversation you have will be filling out the personality of the community on which you have statistics.

If you have children, you will also want to visit schools at the grade levels they will be entering. You can call ahead for an appointment if you specifically wish to speak to the principal, but appointments are not really necessary. If you stop at the school's central office and explain to the secretary that you will be moving to the area and would like to talk with someone about the school, there is almost always someone available to give you a tour and answer your questions. Remember, a teacher, a guidance counselor, the school librarian, or sometimes even a student can give you just as many valuable insights as the principal. (Sometimes more.)

As you tour the school plant, ask the questions that are important to you. Do you want to know what extracurricular activities are available? How children are grouped in the classroom? Where school district lines run and how the children get to and from school? Is discipline important to you? How is it enforced?

While you're walking and talking, keep your eyes open. How do the children behave in class, between classes, and on the playground? Are the hallways and lavatories clean and free of graffiti? Is there an adequate cafeteria, auditorium, gym? Is the library books only, or does it contain magazines, videotapes, computer programs, games, perhaps even a conference area? And, finally, ask yourself, would you like to go to school here? Take notes and take away with you any printed matter the school might have to describe itself.

On Location

If you are buying rather than renting your living space, there's a little more to choosing your new hometown than matching its personality with yours. There's the question of money. Most Americans want a home and an investment property all wrapped up into one. Well, nothing influences the investment value of your living space more than its location.

Location equals town, neighborhood, and lot. We'll get to neighborhood and lot in the next chapter—right now, let's look at the factors that influence appreciation potential in a given community.

Before there were bricks and mortar, before there was money, even before there were lawyers, there was the essential economic barometer: supply and demand. If the demand for housing in a given area is higher than the supply, prices will go up. (So will rents.) If supply exceeds demand, prices will stagnate or begin to lose ground relative to inflation. Knowing and *using* this basic bit of economic information can make the difference between real profit in your housing investment or merely a hedge against inflation.

Now is the time to look beyond the preferred cities the computer printed out for you. Get information on the socioeconomic picture for the whole area. Where are the major employers? Is the area saturated with only one industry or are there several? Are new employers moving into the area? Are the established ones expanding?

Once you pinpoint where the jobs are, check out transportation facilities to these locations. Find out where major rail and bus routes stop—good public transportation usually increases property value. Get a highway map and check out the current and proposed routes in your area. Buying within a few miles of a highway about to be completed can mean a big jump in property value (as long as your property doesn't actually abut, overlook, or lie within sound and smoke distance of the road, that is).

If an area looks inviting and business is booming, collect information on housing construction. A good real estate agent can tell you who is building where. Often an area becomes economically hot and prices begin to spiral. Builders, being no fools, buy and begin developing land. Everyone wants to make maximum money, so housing expands quickly, and before you know it, overbuilding has created a supply that exceeds demand. So be sure that there isn't *too* much residential building going on before you buy into an area.

If the towns on your preferred list coincide with the towns you see as having the greatest potential for housing appreciation, you have no problem. Just choose the best-for-you among them. If, however, you see one or two towns that you think have great home investment potential but their profiles for education, recreation, community spirit, or whatever-is-important-to-you are less than some of the other communities in the area, you must choose, giving priority to money or happiness. This isn't always easy.

Personally, I favor an answer based on future plans. If you're planning to remain in an area more or less indefinitely, you might just as well choose happiness and settle down in the town that most closely fits your personality preferences. If you know you'll be transferred within three to five years, on the other hand, and you think an area will catch fire economically during that time (the interstate highway will be complete in eighteen months, for example), you might want to sacrifice some of your happiness for the short-term goal of making a killing on your home investment. You can then use the profits to get you into a perfect, or almost perfect, town on your next move.

After supply and demand, the quality of the local schools and the services for the property tax dollar seem to be most important in influencing the cost of housing in a town. Towns with good schools, good municipal services, and low taxes usually have housing prices that are relatively high for the area. Shopping, recreation facilities, and personal services such as hospitals, day-care centers, and religious and cultural groups are other factors in adding to housing value in a community.

Predicting the Future

If making money is a part of your motivation to own your own home, and if you know or suspect that you'll probably be transferred again, a crystal ball would be a big help in choosing your hometown. Where will housing appreciate fastest? No one can answer that question infallibly. But there are some indicators that you can use to help you predict where prices are going in the next few years.

The first, of course, is what's happened in the past few years. Go to the local libraries in the towns you are considering and ask for issues of the local newspaper from a year or two ago. Turn to the real estate sections and compare the asking prices on similar homes in yesterday's and last year's newspapers. This will give you a rather accurate idea of how housing is appreciating in each town. You might also ask the real estate agent you are working with if he or she has comparables available from two years back, or even from last year. Compare the actual selling prices of houses sold over a year ago with the selling prices of houses sold a month or two ago. You may not know what the market will do next year, but at least you'll know what it has done. And very often the past is a prediction of the future.

Then ask the real estate agent if there is any major retail sales construction going on in the area. Look specifically for grocery chains, fast food franchises, home supply centers, huge department or discount stores, shopping malls. Construction of really large shopping facilities in or near a residential area usually indicates expected population and economic growth. Shopping center developers and major retail chains don't just pick any spot to build their malls. They issue checks with lots of zeros on them to research firms who do extensive market studies before any land is purchased. So if there is major commercial construction going on in an area, you can usually bet on better-than-average housing appreciation.

Be advised, however, that the house with a backyard that abuts the parking lot of the new A&P is very hard to sell. Almost as difficult as the house with the living room picture window that pictures only traffic on the new interstate.

Your Lifestyle Preferences

Have each person who is moving with you rate the following items on a scale of 1 to 10.

$$1 = \text{Not important at all}$$
$$10 = \text{Of utmost importance}$$

Length of commute to work	———
Public transportation	———
Good public schools	———
Private or religious schools	———
Adult educational opportunities	———
Medical and personal services	———
Child-care facilities	———
Youth recreation groups	———
Youth athletic programs	———
Parks and open spaces	———
Hobby and special interest groups	———
Good public library	———
Good shopping	———
Theater, music, and movies	———
Restaurants	———
Community service activities	———
Religious groups	———
Ethnic groups	———
Self-help groups	———
Gardening opportunities	———
Laws that govern the keeping of pets	———

CHAPTER 8

Choosing Your Next Living Space

"WHAT'S THE PROBLEM?" you ask. "You look for a four-bedroom, two-and-a-half-bath Colonial, preferably with a fireplace in the family room. Oh, and a three-car garage would be nice, too."

Yes, if you fit the profile of one particular group of Americans. That is, if you're married, have two or more kids, a dog or maybe two cats, and a riding mower that you enjoy for an hour or more each weekend. But not everyone fits that slot, or wants to. Housing style is a very personal choice, and the closer your choice fits your personality, the happier you are likely to be living in it.

Let me go over the housing options readily available to Americans today, with some plus and minus factors noted. *Your* task will be to choose the pluses that are most important to you and the minuses that you can live with.

American Housing

THE SUBURBAN TRACT HOME

In the forty years that followed World War II, single family tract housing was the most common type of residential construction in the United States. That distinction is being challenged today by the condominium community, not because home-buyers like condos better (they don't), but because many people can't afford the price tag on single family houses and because builders make more money building condos.

A suburban tract house might be a four-room Cape Cod on a fifty-by-one-hundred-foot lot or a ten-room contemporary (not counting the master bath suite with its whirlpool tub for two) on three acres of manicured lawn. Besides the usual detached housing advantages of privacy, the potential for garage and storage space, and a little land to enjoy, the greatest advantage of the tract house is the homogeneity of the neighborhood. The houses within a particular development may be carbon copies of each other or there may be great variety in exterior styling (the so-called custom design), but the amount of interior living space is usually within five hundred to nine hundred square feet of each other and the market value rarely varies by more than 15 percent above the value of what had once been the lowest-priced model home.

The obvious advantage of this homogeneity is value protection. It's almost as good as investing in triple-A municipal bonds. Any appraiser will find it easy to work for you, there are comparables all around, and nothing is likely to change drastically.

There is another, less tangible, advantage to tract house homogeneity, however. The similar house prices and styles tend to attract similar types of people, and you will find yourself living among neighbors pretty much like yourself. This can be a big advantage for people relocating in a new area of the country, for it facilitates making new friends. In fact, many such neighborhoods actually have standing welcome groups and regularly scheduled get-togethers. You'll also find it easier in a tract development to find other people like yourself who might be willing to exchange baby-sitting time or join a car pool for the kids' soccer practices.

Among the disadvantages of suburban tract house living is a complete dependence on your car for transportation. There's rarely a bus line that stops anywhere near Sprawling Acres, and even a corner store where you can buy bread and milk is a rarity. The commute to work is also usually long, although that fact has changed recently in some areas where major corporations are relocating some or all of their office space in suburbia, along major interstates.

Most important of all, however, the suburban house demands time and more time, eats up a great deal of money, or both. You, its owner, have all the responsibility for keeping the grass cut, the hedges trimmed, the snow and ice off the sidewalk and driveway, the house painted, the gutters and downspouts free of leaves, the furnace in good repair, the septic tank cleaned, and the interior looking lovely. You even have to get the squirrel out of the attic or pay someone to do it for you. This feature of suburban living means that you either develop handyman skills rather quickly or become prepared to spend a relatively large portion of your income on home maintenance.

If you choose to rent a suburban tract house, you will almost surely get more space for your rental dollar than if you were to rent an apartment. But you will probably be required to keep the lawn mowed and the sidewalks shoveled. You will share with your neighbors all the advantages and disadvantages of living in Sprawling Acres except that your monthly payment won't be building equity and you won't be responsible for repairs if the old oak tree is struck by lightning and comes through the roof.

THE SUBURBAN OLDER HOME OR CUSTOM HOME

You see yourself as an individualist and you want your home to reflect your unique personality. You want the grace and charm of a circular stairway and carved walnut moldings. Or perhaps you want a master bedroom loft with skylights and a balcony that overlooks the living room with its floor-to-ceiling fieldstone fireplace. What you're looking for will probably be either quite new, built within the past five years, or quite old, built more than fifty years ago.

Besides individuality, quality workmanship is a goal that many home-buyers in this group seek and often find. Home pride is important to them, and they take joy in detail and beauty rather than seeking out functionality and convenience.

The disadvantages of new or old custom-designed homes are price and maintenance costs. But if money is not a problem in your life, these are hardly disadvantages. The question of investment value, however, may show itself when you attempt to sell such a property. The unusual home is difficult to appraise and must often wait long on the market for the right buyer to come along.

Before choosing to buy an older home, you should evaluate the surrounding buildings carefully, since their condition and use will have an effect on the value of your property. Before buying a newer custom-built home or contracting to have one built for you, you should look carefully at all the open land nearby. Go to the municipal zoning office and look at the town's master plan. How is the open land near the property you are considering zoned? What is likely to be built there and how will that construction affect the value of your home? And, remember, zoning *can* be changed.

If you choose a large, older home, your commute to work might be eased by the availability of public transportation, and walking to the grocery store may just become your daily exercise. If you choose a newly built custom home that is remotely located, however, you'll again be completely dependent upon your car. Security may also be a problem since there will be no neighborhood watch group. And you will find it harder to make friends within the community, since you will not have a neighborhood as a starting point.

Only occasionally will you find a custom home or a large older home for rent. Most investors who buy houses with the plan of renting them in the interim before selling becomes profitable buy tract houses or small urban houses. The large, old, gracious home represents too much maintenance work and requires too specialized a buyer to interest an investor. Few, therefore, are for rent, except perhaps by the occasional owner who must leave on a temporary transfer. Newer custom-built homes are too expensive to be good investment property.

THE URBAN DETACHED HOUSE

Again we're talking about older houses here, since most of the urban land available for residential development filled up years ago. And land that is being redeveloped in urban centers today is almost exclusively devoted to multiunit housing. So if you want a detached house in an urban setting, you are choosing a maintenance problem. You should allow for extra expenditures in your budget or learn a bunch of handyman skills as quickly as possible.

Parking may also be a problem if you want to keep a car in the city. Many city properties are built so close to each other that there are no driveways or garages. You must park on the street, which can be a problem in every snowstorm and an invitation to theft and vandalism, or you must rent garage space for your car. On the other hand, you may not need to own a car (or certainly not two cars) if you choose this housing option, since urban transportation will be available to you.

Assuming a minuscule lot, you'll be free from the Saturday-morning commitment to lawn maintenance that plagues suburban homeowners, but finding safe and adequate play areas for your children may pose a problem. If you have or intend to have children, scout for nearby parks and playgrounds or buildings that house youth recreation centers before you buy.

You'll find a much greater diversity of people in urban neighborhoods. There will almost certainly be a wide spectrum in age, including some old people who have owned their homes for forty years or more. There might also be an ethnic core. There will probably be yuppies, some of whom will probably be tenants. There will be some singles, some single parents, and some empty-nesters. There will probably be some two-career married couples with latchkey children, and you may even find a live-in mother-in-law or two.

There is a fair amount of rental property available among urban houses. If you choose to rent this type of living space, you share the same advantages and disadvantages as the urban homeowner, but again without the benefits of growing equity and federal income tax deductions.

THE MULTIFAMILY HOUSE

If money (the shortage thereof) is a consideration in your housing hunt and you would like to get into homeownership, you might well consider buying a multifamily house. The mortgage lender will consider the rental income from the unit or units that you do not occupy in qualifying you for a mortgage, and multifamily houses generally sell for slightly less than comparable space in a single family house.

The advantages of this housing style are quite obviously the income from the rental units and the opportunity for federal income tax savings. Its disadvantages are the need to share your yard space with your tenants, the lack of privacy inherent in living within the same building as other people not related to you, and the general duties of the landlord: collecting the rents, keeping the books, doing maintenance work, and generally keeping order.

Most multifamily houses are within urban areas and transportation is not as serious a problem as it is in suburban tract houses. Children can also walk to some activities and even to after-school sitters or extended-time child-care facilities. In fact, choosing this housing style may considerably cut down your in-the-car time.

If you are a tenant, you can usually rent more space for your money in a multifamily than in an apartment house. The disadvantages are loss of anonymity, lack of services such as a super or doorman, and sometimes a less-than-optimum location.

THE HANDYMAN SPECIAL

If making money is one of your chief motivations in finding a new living space, consider the handyman special. Find the worst-decorated, most run-down place in a good area and buy it. Be sure that it is structurally sound, however, because buckling basement walls or an improperly built roof could wipe out all your potential profit.

Be aware when you choose a handyman special that you are making a time and money commitment. You will spend most of your weekends on "the house," everything will take longer than you expected, and you will have to pour a good deal of your pocket money into buying things like doorstops, switch boxes, paint, and floor covering.

Choosing a good neighborhood and town is essential to your moneymaking success in this housing style. If there is only one run-down house in the neighborhood (yours), go ahead and buy. The condition of the rest of the area will safeguard your investment. If there are many run-down houses, however, you need to do some serious study. Is the neighborhood going up or down? Are more people buying and rehabbing houses than are buying them and letting them go to seed?

One of the criteria used by professional investors to judge secure investment potential in a handyman special is the proportion of owner-occupants in the neighborhood. If most of the property owners live elsewhere, house values in the neighborhood are unlikely to be going up. Another consideration is the character of the surrounding streets. Your best bet is to choose a property in the middle of a residential area that is fully developed. This will prevent a massage parlor from opening up next door and rubbing away your potential profits.

CREATIVE CONVERSIONS

You say you heard about some people who bought an abandoned church and turned it into a beautiful house that they sold for four times the amount they paid in less than three years. And you want to do that yourself.

Okay. But it takes perseverance to find a place with the potential for conversion, a creative mind to see the possibilities, some real estate savvy and experience to understand the implications of zoning laws and building codes, and sometimes the help of an architect. Barns, defunct gas stations, boathouses, movie theaters, etc., simply were not designed for human habitation. It will take skill, time, and money to do the conversion. Will you be able to live there while the work is going on? Legally? And when your dream conversion is completed and you are ready to move on to a different kind of housing, will you be able to sell it?

Consider the neighborhood. It's unlikely to be the nice suburban tract that draws large numbers of prospective home-buyers. In fact, exactly what kind of buildings are there near your creative conversion? Housing in the midst of a commercial area is very hard to sell. So is housing in the middle of nowhere!

In fact, most creative conversions are hard to sell no matter how beautiful they are. Are you willing to put in the time required to do the conversion and then live there for many years? Or are you planning to live with sawdust on your toast just long enough to finish the work?

One couple I know hoped to make a fortune by converting a barn. They filed for divorce while the project was in process and then finally resolved their dispute by taking out a loan to have the conversion completed professionally. They still live in their barn/house and are very proud of it.

CONDOMINIUMS

Is there someone out there somewhere who doesn't know what a condominium is? Since the end of the seventies, they have been the fastest-growing sector of the housing marketplace. And today they come in all shapes and sizes. There's the high-rise, the mid-rise, and the low-rise. Or you can have garden-style, or perhaps a theme community such as F. Scott Fitzgerald Land or Mr. Spock (of the pointed ears) Village. You can even have a condominium community of single family detached houses. How? Each person owns the structure in which he or she lives and an undivided interest in the land and recreational facilities.

Condominiums are a kind of property ownership in which you own fee simple certain carefully defined space. Now this may just be the airspace within certain walls or it may be an entire structure on certain ground. Along with your ownership of certain space, you also hold an undivided interest in the ownership of shared facilities. These facilities may be walls, staircases, swimming pools, tennis courts, parking areas, roads, golf courses, the basement, the roof, the heating plant, the elevators. You get the idea.

When you own an undivided interest in something, you own a share, but you cannot separate that share from the whole. You cannot take a single brick out of the building or a chair out of the recreation area. Almost by definition, therefore, you are an owner subject to the rules that are enacted for the good of the community. These rules are the bylaws of the condominium association. They are enforced by the board of directors, a group that is elected, usually from among the owners, to oversee the functioning (financial and physical) of the condominium community.

Laws that govern pets, children, use of the pool, parking areas, the rental of units, landscaping, even the color of your front door, appear in most condominium documents. Common areas of the condominium community are maintained by contributions (not voluntary—*assessments* is actually a better word) from the condominium unit owners. These assessments are commonly called maintenance fees. Unlike local property tax assessments, however, they are not deductible on federal income tax returns.

Just about every condominium community has an owners' association in which each unit owner holds a given number of votes. That number is usually determined by the relative value of his or her condominium unit. A two-bedroom apartment will carry more votes than a one-bedroom unit. An apartment near the pool might have more votes than one near the sewerage pumping station. A townhouse on the fourth tee would be valued more highly than one next door to the maintenance building.

The advantage of condominium living is freedom from outdoor maintenance chores. All that work is done by a maintenance staff or the company that the board of directors hires. Of course, you pay for this freedom from work in your maintenance fee, but the cost is considerably lower than you would pay to have your suburban house's lawn maintained.

The disadvantages of condominium living that most people complain about are the proximity of other people (it's just like living in an apartment complex, some say, and it is); the necessity to share space (it can be very aggravating to arrive home at 1:00 A.M. and find someone parked in your parking slot); and the strictness of condominium rules (no pets was fine until you fell in love with that miniature poodle).

Condominiums also do not sell quite as well or appreciate quite as quickly as single family houses. They do afford a good way to break into a community, however, since there are usually recreational facilities on the premises where you can meet your neighbors. The owners' association, with its many committees, is also an excellent way to get to know other condominium owners by working with them.

Many apartments in condominium communities are owned by investors and are available for rent. So be sure to check out condominiums if you are apartment-hunting.

CO-OP APARTMENTS

Co-op apartments are found in scattered areas around the country, mostly larger cities and mostly in older buildings that were once rental apartment buildings but have been converted to co-op ownership. New York City has the largest number of co-ops in the nation, with Miami and Washington next in line. Owning a co-op is more or less like owning a condominium except that you don't really own real estate. Instead, you own stock in the corporation that owns the building and you have a proprietary lease that allows you to occupy your apartment.

There are even more rules in a co-op building than in a condominium community. You can't even put up a wall to divide one room into two in a co-op without the permission of the board of directors, since you don't own the inside of your apartment. For all intents and purposes, you are a tenant with an ownership share in the building. You can, of course, sell your co-op apartment, but be aware that some co-op corporations require that the buyers be approved by the board of directors and that approval can be refused for any reason except those specifically prohibited by law, such as race or religion. This approval process could hold up your sale for many months.

Even though co-op owners don't really own real estate, they are entitled to homeowner-type tax deductions on federal income tax returns as long as their building remains primarily residential. Otherwise, choosing a co-op is pretty much like choosing a condominium or even renting an apartment.

MOBILE HOMES

The people who build these don't want them to be called mobile homes anymore since 97 percent of the structures never get moved from their first location. The now-accepted terminology is *manufactured housing*, but most people still refer to them as mobiles.

Do you want to live in one? You may be thinking of the community of roadside silver shoeboxes you used to drive by when you were a kid. Well, few of those remain. The newer manufactured home communities are quite different, with parking areas, recreation facilities, and a variety of quite appealing dwellings. Rental in these communities can be comparatively inexpensive and may well hold you over until you can become accustomed to an area and decide where it is you really want to live.

Many manufactured homes are actually owned by their inhabitants. If you choose to buy in a mobile home park that has both rental and ownership units, your appreciation will not be as good as it might be in other real estate investments. If, however, you choose to have a manufactured house set on a foundation on a piece of land that you buy, you can finance it just like any other house, and its appreciation will probably keep pace with the local market. The bonus is that manufactured housing costs about 40 percent less than comparable housing that is built on site.

RENTAL APARTMENT BUILDINGS

If you want anonymity, total flexibility, and freedom from maintenance chores, or if you simply don't have the money to buy, renting in a large building or garden-style complex may be your housing of choice. There is little money at risk here. If you make a poor choice and decide to move out, you might lose your security deposit, but that's usually it. The real risk of a poor choice is in time and happiness. You could rent in what you later discover to be a very inconvenient location. Or you might dislike the people you share your building with. Or you may wish you had spent just a little more to get access to a pool and tennis courts. So don't just take the first place you see, thinking it doesn't really matter. It does.

Choose an area of town where you really want to live, close to the things that are important to you. Then spend some time in the apartment buildings you are considering. These communities have personalities, too. What kind of people are living there? Young? Old? Lots of children? No children? Pets? Is there a predominant ethnic group? Is there a gathering place, or do most people meet in the laundry room? Does the building have a newsletter? You can learn a lot by reading an issue or two.

You want to find a place where you will fit in, feel comfortable, as soon as possible, and a place that will meet your housing needs. If you have a car, you will want an apartment complex that guarantees you a parking space. If a health club is important to you, see if you can find an apartment building or complex that has one on the premises so you won't have to pay to join a private club and go out at night to use it. If security is important to you, find an apartment building or complex that has a doorman or a gateman.

Moneymaking Potential

If you are renting, the convenience and comfort you get for your money are your only concerns. If you are buying, however, you want the money that you invest in a home to be safe. And safety is a question of location.

After the town, the neighborhood is the most important factor in determining the value of your property. If you are shown a neighborhood of 1950s split-levels and you buy the *only* brand-new four-bedroom Colonial there, your house will never be worth a great deal more than the others around it, even if it would sell for twice the price in a neighborhood of houses like itself. Neighborhood is that important in determining value.

The same goes for additions. Even if the sellers of a house have spent $70,000 on a two-story addition, the house is unlikely to sell for more than 15 percent above the going price in the neighborhood.

If you know you will be moving again in a few years and you want to be able to sell quickly and well, choose a house that is not unusual and one that is in the middle of the price range for the neighborhood. Try to avoid buying on the fringes of a neighborhood or tract development when the character of nearby property is of lesser value or zoned for commercial use. Properties that abut "open spaces" land or recreational facilities such as parks or golf courses usually bring higher prices. Backing up to a school yard, however, will lower the value and salability of a property. So will backing up to the parking lot of a shopping center, a highway, a railroad track, any commercial establishment, a hospital, a fire-house, a prison, or a police station.

The size, shape, and contour of your lot will also affect the value of your property. Generally, a little extra land will get you a little extra money. Seven acres of swamp behind your house, however, may actually get you less money. Who wants to pay taxes on unusable land? The owner of such land would do better to deed the swampy part to the town for open spaces and collect his or her tax break.

Try to select lots that are regular in shape. Squares and rectangles are generally best. Pie-shaped or irregular lots usually hold back a sale unless there is some particularly attractive reason for the unusual shape, a lake or a mountain, for example. Corner lots also sell less quickly in the residential real estate marketplace even though they sell more quickly in the commercial marketplace. Flat or nearly flat lots are more desirable to the general public than lots that fall off or climb steeply from the roadbed. Upside from the road is somewhat more desirable than downside, however.

Avoid lots with streams that run through them. You may think the babbling brook is cute, but many buyers are wary of water running through their land. And with good reason. I've seen a gurgling rivulet turn into a river so rapid and powerful that it carried the trunk of a tree through a picture window and into the living room. The incident sticks in my mind because we almost bought that house but finally discounted it *because* of the running water. Two years later, it had the tree in its living room.

Good traffic patterns within a house are essential to resale value. For this reason, many houses with additions do not sell well, especially if the addition creates a traffic pattern that forces you to walk through one room to get into another. The only exception to the walk-through rule is the kitchen. A kitchen at the center of the house is not a detriment to a sale.

Closets and storage are also important. And light is a positive feature everywhere. Long hallways are a negative. Wet basements are a definite deterrent.

Among today's most fashionable home features are: master bathrooms that resemble health spas; skylights; a library, study, or computer room on the main floor; ceramic tile countertops in the kitchen; and center island stovetops, especially if they can be converted to a barbecue grill. Breakfast nooks, preferably south-facing with lots of hanging plants, will impress most buyers. Three-car garages are a common feature in new luxury construction. Central air conditioning is a major selling point. Porches are back, especially front porches!

If you are buying a condominium, the location of your unit within the complex can be important in determining resale value. Many people like the outer edges of a garden-type community, especially if there is designated green space around the borders of the condominium community's land. A high location is most valuable in a high-rise, but wherever you are in the building, avoid buying units near trash chutes and elevators. Corner apartments are particularly desirable.

If you can wait for its completion, choosing to have a house built for you in a tract development that is just opening up is often one of the best financial investments a home-buyer can make. Most builders consciously price the first few houses that are to be built on the low side of market value to get people attracted to the area. Once several homes are up and occupied, even if their front lawns are mud and rocks, prices in the development go up. The one time that my husband and I had a new house built for us, we were the first to buy in the area. The value of that house had doubled—yes, doubled—by the time we put the deck on three years later.

Another good buy is the less-than-one-year-old house of a person unexpectedly being transferred out of the area, especially if new construction is still going on in that development. During the course of the first year, the sellers have usually done all the landscaping work, and a great deal of decorating. You will probably find wall-to-wall carpeting and draperies inside and many of the other extras every new-home buyer puts in at out-of-pocket cost. The price of this still new, but now well-polished, house will be capped, however, by the asking price for houses under construction in the development. The cost of all the first-year extras usually amounts to considerably more than the price hike on the builder's models. As the tract later nears completion, you'll be chalking up the profits brought about by the builder's continuing price hikes. And the extras you paid nothing for will make the house more valuable yet.

Working with a Real Estate Agent

Just as in choosing your new hometown, the information that you give to the real estate agent will determine much of the ease and success of your hunt for a suitable living space. Above all, be honest. You will need to provide the agent with two kinds of information: financial and personal.

If you are renting, tell the agent what you want to spend per month. If you are buying, it's a little more complicated. How much down payment do you have? How much mortgage are you qualified to carry? Those two answers, along with the taxes on specific properties, will determine which properties you can buy. It's all right to look at places a bit above your limit; most sellers do come down. But don't reach too far or you'll waste time looking at dream houses you can't afford and everything you can afford will pale in comparison.

Just as you prepared a preference profile to assist in your choice of a new hometown, prepare a "need" and "want" list to help in choosing a living space. The "need" column should be a list of absolute essentials. If you have four children, you need at least three bedrooms. The "want" column should be a list of things you'd like but might be willing to sacrifice for something else. It should be prioritized with the items you want most and are least willing to give up at the top and the most tradable items at the bottom.

In many areas of the country, your real estate agent will take the figures that you have calculated as your price range and the features from your need and want list and type them into the office computer. The printer will then supply you with a list of properties just right for you. This is a good beginning, but not the whole picture. Computer print-outs are not easy to read, and one can get confused sorting through "houses" that are only words typed on paper.

The MLS book or cards that the real estate agent uses are a good means of checking through the computer's suggestions. They invariably have pictures, which help, and the listings are arranged by price so you can see what else is available that the computer didn't pick in the same price range.

If there is a multiple listing system in the area in which you are house-hunting, use one real estate agent only. If you don't like the one you're with, change, but don't work with three or four in the same area. You'll only waste a lot of time making your likes and dislikes known to each agent, and you will surely be taken to some of the same properties more than once. If you see a property that interests you advertised in the newspaper, call *your* agent, even though it appears under another broker's name. Your agent can get you whatever information you want and can arrange a showing.

On the other hand, if you are looking in several different towns ten miles or more apart, use a separate agent for each town. As I've said before, real estate is really a local business. You want your agent to be an expert in the area in which you are looking. No one can be an expert in a radius of fifty miles!

If the real estate agent offers to show you videos of the houses you have chosen, do look at them, but don't discount a house because you find the video distasteful. Videos have their limitations. You can't really get the feel of a place by watching it on a screen. Go through everything that meets your needs. Try to discount decorating and dirt. But do check out condition. Some factors such as peeling paint, especially exterior paint, broken windows, poor plumbing or wiring, leaking roofs, termites, overgrown landscaping, and water in the basement are negotiating points for major reductions in price. Most can be fixed, however.

When you do decide on a property, be sure to have a professional home inspection service go through it for you. Make your contract contingent upon a satisfactory report. Do this even if you are buying a condominium, or perhaps especially if you are buying a condominium, since the home inspector can get access to places in the building or complex where you ordinarily wouldn't be allowed to go. A broken elevator or run-down heating plant can mean a huge expenditure in the near future, which will mean a higher maintenance fee next year when you own a unit.

Head and Heart Again

In the home-selling chapters, I cautioned you repeatedly to be rational and not allow your heart to get into the marketing of or negotiating over your home. Now I want to change my tune a bit. When you are looking for a living space, it's important that you love the place you choose at least a little. If you don't, if you just settle for something available and affordable, you may find yourself moving sooner than is necessary. And as you surely know, that's expensive.

On the other hand, your heart should not rule untethered. When you fall in love with a property, try out my "headstrong" exercise. Do not make an offer the first time you see it. Instead, go back to your hotel room, separate if there are two of you, and each try to draw a floor plan of this property that you love. Allow yourself twenty minutes' drawing time.

You are going to be surprised at how much you don't remember. When twenty minutes have passed, get together and compare your floor plans. Don't be upset if they don't match; they probably won't. It doesn't matter who is right and who is wrong. The idea of the exercise is to get you thinking rationally about the property without the influence of decorating, or the view, or the beautiful blue carpeting in the living room to detract you.

Make a list of questions that come up during your discussion of your floor plan drawings. Then go back to the property again with your floor plans in hand and a clean sheet of paper to draw a new one. In your new drawing, don't forget windows, closets, doorways, and storage places. Also sketch the lot if a copy of the survey is not available. How much yard work is there likely to be?

If you still love the place after doing my headstrong exercise, you are ready to make an offer. Now your negotiating skills will be called upon. The next chapter will help you.

CHAPTER 9

Making an Offer

IF YOU HAVE EVER LIVED in Morocco, Mexico, or any of the other countries in the world where people routinely bargain over the price of whatever they buy, you are far better prepared for the real estate negotiating process than most Americans. With the possible exception of the automobile marketplace, the art of discussing price is but rarely practiced in the United States. Some Americans actually believe that the price printed on the real estate agent's listing form is the amount of money the owner expects to get for the property. It almost never is. The job of the savvy home-buyer is to find the lowest price that the seller will accept.

"Well, that's an easy one," you suggest. "Just make a ridiculously low offer and see what they say."

No! No! In fact, really low first offers have been known to antagonize some sellers to the point where they refuse to negotiate further with the people who made the offer. Now this is a foolish move, I agree, but it does happen.

"So what do you do?" you ask. "Just offer them a couple of thousand under asking price? That sounds almost as foolish!"

It is, unless you're in a super-heated market. No, good negotiating technique requires a little behind-the-scenes work before the first offer is made. The best advice for anyone about to buy real estate is: *Know the local marketplace.* But that's a little difficult if you're moving from another state and you have ten days to find a suitable living space. So if you can't exactly achieve intimacy with the local real estate marketplace, get to know it as well as possible by using marketplace data. In home-buying, this means the comparables files. Yes, the same files your real estate agent back home used to help you to establish the market value of the property you are selling.

Ask your real estate agent in the new area to get out comparables for the kind and price range of property you wish to buy. Spread them out on the table before you. How do their actual selling prices compare with their asking prices? How do selling prices compare with the asking price on "your" house? By doing this exercise, you are trying to establish the fair market value of the property you are considering. It is exactly the same procedure that an appraiser would use.

Once you think you know what the property is probably worth, look at the comps again and note how long each was on the market. This information will give you a feel for the tempo of the marketplace. Is it a fast-paced sellers' market where properties are being snapped up quickly and close to asking price? If so, you won't be holding a lot of trump cards in your negotiating hand. Or are you in a slower-moving buyers' market where houses remain on the market for some time and prices are negotiated significantly downward? If that's the case, you might save many thousands with a few good plays in the negotiating game.

After perhaps an hour working with the comps, you should have a very good idea of the market value of the property you want to buy and you should also have an ideal purchase price in mind. (Of course, that will be a price somewhat lower than your estimate of market value.) You should also have a top-dollar price in mind. This may be slightly higher than the market value figure you arrived at, allowing that your calculations are an estimate, that property tends to appreciate with time, and that the place you want to buy may have some desirable features that make it worth a bit more than its comps. You should carefully make note of these three figures: the ideal price, the probable market value price, and your top-dollar price. Do *not*, however, tell the real estate agent anything about the numbers you have arrived at.

Real estate negotiating is not a bridge game with the agent as your partner. That agent is working for the seller; it's written in the listing contract. What you're playing now is cutthroat poker. If you reveal your hand, you will almost certainly lose. Or, to come out of the metaphor, if you tell your real estate agent that this is only your first offer and you can go higher, believe me, you *will* go higher. If you tell your real estate agent what your top-dollar figure is, you are likely to end up paying that figure for the property.

When you play the real estate negotiating game, make each offer as though you absolutely mean it. Do not reveal what you might or might not do later. Take one step at a time and respond only to the seller's response, not to what the agent says.

Questions and Answers

But whoa! I'm telling you how to play your cards, and you haven't even seen your hand yet. Before you start negotiating, you need still more information. The data on fair market value and the tempo of the local marketplace are only a part of the picture. Now you want to know the following:

Why is the seller selling? If your seller has bought another property, you will probably have a strong negotiating hand even in a fast market. No one wants to carry two mortgages if he or she can help it. If your seller is retiring and doesn't quite know where to yet, your negotiating game could be long and involved. There is little seller motivation to get it over. If your seller is a divorcing couple, expect complications. People in the throes of a divorce fight over the most trivial things. If your seller is having a new house built, try to find out where and go to see it. This is not a time-wasting *ahhh* and *oooh* trip; you want to know how far along the building process is so that you can use occupancy date as part of your negotiating.

How long has the property been on the market? If the answer you get is less than a month, you may have to negotiate long and hard to bring down the price beyond a token drop. During the first thirty days or so on the market, most sellers still think they're going to make a killing. If the house has been on the market for some time, you will have a lot of negotiating power.

Have there been any other offers? Real estate agents are required to answer this question truthfully in most states. But don't worry if an offer higher than your top-dollar price was refused six weeks ago. Make your first offer at or just below your ideal price and work toward your estimate of market value anyway. Much changes in the mind of a seller in six weeks.

Has the seller indicated an occupancy date? Most sellers do not state the hoped-for occupancy date on their listings, but a phone call and a few questions from your agent might get you this information. If you can get it, use it as a negotiating tool. If the seller wants a quick closing and offers you immediate occupancy, name a closing date in your first offer that is distant (ninety days or more if your plans allow for this kind of flexibility). Then you can move the closing date closer in time in lieu of more cash or with only a small increment in your offer. Of course, the opposite is true also. If the seller wants or needs to stay in his property for three or more months, stipulate a quick closing in your first offer and then move the closing closer toward your seller's optimum time in lieu of more money.

What extras are included in the sale? These are usually noted on the listing sheet and they should be named in writing again on your contract to purchase. But there may be other little items on the property that you covet, perhaps that fabulous chandelier, or the snowblower in the garage, or the patio furniture, or the designer doghouse. Do not list these extra extras with your first offer. If you get the property at that price, you can afford to buy them new. As you raise your offer, however, begin to include the unlisted extras you want. You are much more likely to get them if you tag them onto an increase in your offering price.

Step by Step

The very worst way to make an offer in the real estate marketplace is to have the agent call the seller on the phone and say, "Will you take $_____?" The answer is almost always no, the offer is not taken seriously, and you, the buyer, learn nothing about the negotiating tactics of the seller.

Offers are most often made by phone when the real estate agent doesn't believe he or she has a chance for an agreement. It's much easier to call and get past this negotiating step than it is to go to the property, sit down with the seller, and present a low first offer. You should insist, therefore, that your offer be presented *in person* even if the agent is saying to you: "This is insane. They'll throw me out of the house! I know they won't take it. Can't you come up a little more?"

Just say, "That's our offer."

This first offer should be below the fair market value figure you decided upon while looking at the comps. How much below will depend upon your evaluation of the tempo of the local marketplace and the seller's desire to sell. It should be a written offer with the terms of the sale (closing date, mortgage contingency, inspection contingency, etc.) spelled out. Most agents will want you to put this information on a standardized contract of sale and sign it. Be aware that if the seller accepts this first offer and also signs the contract, you have bought a house. There's no going back. Unless . . .

Unless you include in your contract an attorney review clause. This clause is mandatory in all real estate contracts in some states, but it can be included on a contract in any state. Your clause might read:

Either the Buyer or the Seller may elect to have an attorney review this contract. If either party consults an attorney, the attorney must complete his or her review of the contract within a three-day period. The three days will be counted from the date of the delivery of the signed contract to the Buyer and the Seller. Do not count Saturdays, Sundays, or legal holidays. The Buyer and the Seller may agree in writing to extend the three-day period for attorney review. This contract will be legally binding at the end of the review period unless an attorney for the Buyer or the Seller disapproves of the contract. If an attorney for the Buyer or the Seller reviews and disapproves of this contract for any reason, that attorney must notify the other party named in the contract within the three-day or agreed-upon period. Upon such notification, the contract is considered terminated and all deposit monies are to be returned to the Buyer.

If you include a clause such as this in your offering contract, you are *not* required to use the services of an attorney, but the option is available if you need or want it. Remember, the attorney review clause can get you out of a deal that you are having nightmares over!

Some real estate agents use a short contract form or something they call a binder during the negotiating, switching to a "real" contract after all the points have been agreed upon. This may sound like a good idea to you until you realize that the agent's "short form" could become a legally binding contract. To avoid this possibility, print on the bottom of the form, but above your signatures, something like:

This agreement is subject to a mutually agreeable contract to be drawn within three business days of its date.

It is common real estate practice throughout the United States that your signed offer to purchase must be accompanied by a check. The amount is usually $1,000, and it is called earnest money, hand money, or good faith money. It is intended to show that you are serious in your desire to purchase the property. You should make the check payable to the real estate firm that is making the offer, followed by a comma and the word *trustee.*

The agent is supposed to show this check to the seller to document that the offer is from a real buyer and made in good faith. Which is all well and good. Problems sometimes come up, however, when negotiations go beyond the first round, which they often do. Some real estate agencies then routinely deposit the earnest money check in their trust account even though there has been no agreement between seller and buyer. If the deal is never made after such a deposit, you, the prospective buyer, will get your money back, but not without considerable delay.

If you come to a dead end in your negotiating, are in town for a week only, and don't have extra thousand-dollar bills lying around in your checking account, the earnest money check deposit policy could create an exasperating situation. You will need to write another check for $1,000 in order to make an offer on another property. Now, if you make the second property offer with the same real estate firm, they can cover for you by saying your check has been deposited. But what if your second-choice property is in a different area, where you have been working with a different broker? You'll be forced into the position of writing a check against insufficient funds, which could result in a bad start for your purchase.

The solution to this problem is really quite simple. Tell the real estate agent that you do not want your earnest money check deposited in any account until there has been a meeting of the minds and a signed contract between the seller and the buyer. If the agent tells you it's company policy to deposit all checks immediately, ask to speak to the office manager or the broker in charge. If the broker insists on depositing your check before negotiations are complete, tell him or her that you will go to another broker to do your business. The company policy will almost certainly be relaxed.

With a written offer form and a check in hand, the agent should present your offer to the seller. Within a reasonable length of time, anywhere from an hour to a day, you should have a response. If there is a counteroffer, items will be crossed out on the contract and new numbers or clauses written in. Each of these will be initialed by the seller if he or she has signed the contract. If you agree to the changes, you will need only to place your initials alongside the seller's to have a binding agreement.

Most sellers, however, simply note the changes they want on the contract and then return it without their signatures. This gives you the opportunity to consider the counteroffer. If you find it acceptable, have a new contract drawn with the new data typed in, sign it, and have it presented to the seller. If you wish to make another offer, however, do not allow the agent to scratch out the initialed places again and write in others. Contracts with many initialed changes are difficult to read and often cause confusion and later problems. Have a new contract typed with your new offer and its terms clearly spelled out.

The offer/counteroffer process can theoretically go on indefinitely, but two rounds is pretty typical in most residential deals. In fact, it's a cliché in the real estate business that negotiations that go on too long will fall apart. So try to be realistic in your negotiating.

Do not let the real estate agent push you into moves you do not want to make, however. The old line "There's someone else interested in the house" often still works, even with the most seasoned buyers. Why? Because fear creeps in. Everyone thinks, at least for a moment, "Maybe we'll lose the house. . . ." I don't know what percentage of the "other interested parties" in the real estate marketplace are fictitious, but two buyers for one property at the same time is unusual, except in the very hottest markets.

Tying Up Loose Ends

You're getting tired. "Okay," you say, "once we've agreed upon price, terms, and extras included or excluded, and everyone has signed the contract to purchase, the deal is all set, right?"

That's a logical assumption, but it's not right. You've forgotten the contingencies. Just about every contract has several. The sale is usually contingent upon the buyer being able to obtain financing. It is also usually contingent upon a satisfactory professional home inspection.

Today, most lenders will tell you in their initial interview whether or not you are qualified to carry the mortgage specified in your contract. Be aware, however, that if you apply for less than is specified in the contract, you are waiving the mortgage contingency.

The home inspection contingency is another matter. Many home inspectors find faults both major and minor during their inspections. In fact, in some cases, the arrival of the home inspection report is a time for reopening negotiations. Few buyers actually walk away from a deal because of some fault unless it's virtually irreparable, like a buckling basement wall, but most insist that the faults be repaired or a reduction be made in the price to cover the estimated cost of the repairs. In some instances, the buyer and the seller agree to split the cost.

Besides contingencies, look for the following items in your contract of sale:

- *A clause saying that the property will be left in broom-clean condition.* This doesn't mean that the woodwork will be washed clean, but at least you won't have to take someone else's trash to the dump.

- *A clause saying that the seller assumes all responsibility for maintenance and insurance until the closing.*

- *A clause saying that the buyer will have the right to inspect the premises on the day of the closing.* When you do this, be certain that all the extras you listed in the contract are indeed still in the house. If the moving men are present, be certain that those items that are supposed to stay are not marked for shipping.

- *If the date of occupancy is important to you, a clause saying that time is of the essence.* In many states, the closing date in the contract is regarded as an approximate date, subject to change. This legal leniency may result in sellers who stay on because their new house isn't ready while you live in a cramped hotel room. If you have *time is of the essence* written into the contract, you can insist on that closing date or get a court order for specific performance. Or, if you prefer, you can make some arrangements in the contract for a penalty fee to be charged the sellers for every day they remain in possession of the property after the closing date specified in the contract. Make this fee high ($150 per diem usually works), and your sellers will be prompted to move out with more haste than any court order could stimulate. The per diem fee is deducted directly from the monies to be paid to the sellers at the closing.

With the price agreed upon, the terms satisfactory, and the home inspection over, the place is almost yours. Now all you have to do is get the money to buy it. How to do that is in the next chapter.

CHAPTER 10

Home Financing

DID I SEE you yawn? Okay, I agree, it *is* unlikely that anyone will be bidding for the movie rights to this chapter. But this aspect of the real estate marketplace has become a vine-tangled jungle over the past eight years. If you're not careful, or if you just don't know what you're doing, you might find yourself caught up in a sci-fi film version of a Venus's-flytrap.

Yes, it's that bad. Choosing the wrong financing could cost you many thousands of dollars. It could even cost you your home if you overextend and find yourself in foreclosure proceedings. So get yourself a cup of coffee and come with me on this brief, but very necessary, guided tour.

The Words and What They'll Mean to You

Mortgage. A mortgage is a loan secured by real property. In other words, if you don't pay back the loan, the lender can take your property. State laws and lawyers can complicate the process more than just a bit, but essentially that's it.

Trust deed. This is a means of financing property used extensively in the western part of the country and recently in some areas of the South. There is no mortgage because you don't actually own the property until you pay off the money you borrowed to buy it. For tax and living purposes, however, you can act as though you own it.

When a trust deed, or deed of trust, as it is sometimes called, is used, title to the property is held by a third party (neither the lender nor the borrower). This third party is usually the title insurance company or the escrow company that does the closing.

The borrower is called the trustor. The holder of the title is called the trustee. And the lender is called the beneficiary. It is the lender who benefits from this arrangement because if you don't make the scheduled payments on your loan, a notice of default can be filed and you can lose your home in as little as ninety days. A far cry from the year or more it can take to foreclose a mortgage.

Second mortgage—equity credit line. I don't think a week goes by when a letter from some bank or lending institution doesn't show up in the mail offering us thousands of dollars in equity credit. Loans secured by the equity in your home are the hot item in late-eighties financing. Be careful!

A second mortgage is just like a first mortgage except that in a foreclosure it will be paid off only after the first mortgage has been satisfied. So the lender has a slightly greater risk of not getting back all the money that was loaned. A property can be foreclosed, however, if you are in default on your second mortgage, even though you are faithfully making all the payments on your first mortgage.

Most equity credit lines are really second mortgages. They are dangerous second mortgages, however, and you'll see why immediately if you read the fine print. The interest rate on most of them is tied to some index. It can change monthly, and, in many cases, it has no upward limitations. So if the prime rate zooms to 20 percent, you could find yourself paying 22 percent on the money you've borrowed on the credit line. And there's no grace period on most of these loans. Two days after the payment due date, you'll get a red-bordered envelope with a payment-overdue notice inside. If you don't pay, poof! There goes your credit rating as foreclosure proceedings get under way.

Principal. This is not the ogre who walks the hallways of the high school. It's the amount of money that you borrow to buy your home.

Interest rate. This is the percentage of the principal that you agree to pay the lender each year to thank him for lending you the money.

Term. The opposite of interminable, although it may not seem so. The term is the life-span of the mortgage, the number of years you have before it will be paid out or before you will be required to pay off whatever balance there remains.

Amortization. This is the process of gradually paying off the principal by making regular monthly payments. In the early eighties, some lenders were using negative amortization on fixed-payment but adjustable-rate loans. Whenever the payment fell short of the amount needed to amortize the loan over its term, the shortfall was simply added to the principal. In times of rising interest rates, a borrower might end up owing more than was originally borrowed even after making payments for ten years. Most loans currently being offered do not allow for negative amortization, but the arrangement is not illegal.

Points. Points are really interest paid in advance in order to make the loan more profitable to the lender. One point is 1 percent of the principal. Points are customarily paid at the closing, although some lenders are now requiring one point to be paid when the loan commitment is accepted by the borrowers. If points are customarily being charged by lenders in the area where you are buying, you can deduct the amount you paid as interest in the year you paid it on your federal income tax return. Note, however, that points paid for refinancing a home are not tax deductible in the year they are paid but must be prorated over the life of the loan.

Loan-to-value ratio. The loan-to-value ratio will determine the minimum down payment the lender will allow you to make. Few lenders will lend more than 80 percent of the property's value without mortgage insurance of some kind, either government-sponsored or privately sold.

Mortgage insurance.   Mortgage insurance will not pay off your principal in the event of your death. That's life insurance. Mortgage insurance protects the lender only. If you default on your payments and foreclosure is necessary, mortgage insurance guarantees that the lender will get the entire principal, even if the property sells at a price that will not meet this obligation. Federal Housing Administration and Veterans Administration loans provide the lender with this safety net, which means that loans can be written at 95 percent loan-to-value ratio, or even for 100 percent of the purchase price in the case of VA loans. Most private mortgage insurance requires a down payment of at least 5 percent. Even though mortgage insurance protects the lender, you, the borrower, pay the premiums!

Disclosure requirements.   In 1968, the federal government enacted the Truth-in-Lending Act, which was revised and updated in 1982. Essentially, it requires that the lender provide you with complete and accurate information about the real cost of borrowing money. If you don't understand the truth-in-lending statement that the lender gives you (and some of them seem to be written in Sanskrit), ask the bank officials to explain . . . and explain again until you do understand.

Loan Types

Once upon a time, not so very long ago, there were two "kinds" of home financing available: conventional and government-supported (FHA and VA). Since then, the home financing scene has changed so drastically that the term *conventional mortgage* has pretty much dropped from the vocabulary of the real estate marketplace. Today, we talk of fixed-rate mortgages and adjustables. And even the FHA and VA allow both.

The fixed-rate mortgage, however, is really the old conventional by another name. Its interest rate is fixed on the day you close and will not change during the life of the loan. Your monthly payments may go up because of property tax increases, but your principal and interest payment will not change.

Unless . . . yes, there is an unless in this creative-financing age. The graduated payment mortgage is a fixed-rate mortgage in most instances, but the payments are set up to be lower in the early years of the mortgage, when the borrowers supposedly have less money, and then increase gradually to another fixed figure that will pay out the loan within its term. There's a lot of computerized number-juggling involved here, so if you think such an arrangement might work for you, try to get the advice of a really good accountant or financial adviser to be sure that the numbers are really beneficial to you. Remember, your friendly neighborhood banker no longer exists. Lenders nowadays are corporations intent only on profit.

Today's adjustable mortgages have been the topic of entire books. Up until the mid-1980s, most home-buyers regarded them with justifiable suspicion. "What if interest rates go back to 18 percent?" they asked. "What if we couldn't make the higher payments because of the adjustable interest rate? Would we lose the house?"

When lenders replied, "Well, yes, theoretically you could. But, of course, rates won't go that high again," most home-buyers said, "No, thanks!"

The dust has settled, however, and most of today's adjustables have some built-in safety features for the home-buyer. Not only is the adjustment period specified (one year, two years, three years, even five years), but interest rates are capped. You'll have to read the loan proposal carefully, but the most common arrangements are a 1 to 2 percentage-point maximum increase at each adjustment time, with a lifetime maximum increase of 5 or 6 percentage points. Thus, if you took out a three-year adjustable loan at 9 percent at the time of closing, with a 1 percent cap per adjustment period and a 5 percent lifetime cap, you would face the following worst-case scenario:

After three years, your rate of interest would go to 10 percent. After another three years, it would go to 11 percent. And so on. The highest interest you would ever pay on the loan would be 14 percent, but it would take you fifteen years to get to that rate! Meanwhile, if rates were to go down, most adjustables (or at least any adjustable that you would consider) would also go down. Like the maximum ceiling, however, most adjustables also have a minimum floor interest that you would pay no matter how low rates were to go. But I don't think most of us will have to worry about that in our lifetimes.

If you are considering an adjustable, it is also very important that you ask about the index to which the rate adjustments are tied. The lender is required to give you this information and to show you how that index has performed in relation to other indexes over the past several years. Try to find a lender who will tie in to an index that has not fluctuated widely and has remained on the low side of the interest rate scale.

The "new kid on the block" in the mortgage marketplace is the convertible adjustable. The terms of this loan allow you to convert your adjustable-rate loan to a fixed-rate loan at specified times during the life of the mortgage. The initial interest rate on these convertibles is usually somewhat higher than that of nonconvertible adjustables, but if you think rates might dip and you might be able to lock in that dip as a permanent rate for the rest of your days in that particular property, a convertible adjustable might be your best deal.

Choosing Your Best Bet

Shopping for a mortgage when you're a thousand miles from home can be almost as trying as shopping for a living space. Fortunately, you need not inspect the premises of every lender that has an enticing offering. Let the real estate agent help you and then, as the phone company says, "Let your fingers do the walking."

Most real estate agencies have closets literally filled with printed matter from lenders in the area. Take back to your hotel room as much as you can carry. Then machine-copy the Yellow Pages of the local phone book under the headings "Banks" and "Mortgages." Even after you have returned home, you can fine-tune your mortgage-shopping by calling the lenders listed and asking to speak with someone in the new-mortgages department. Lenders will be happy to send you whatever information is at hand. You do *not* have to apply for a mortgage in order to get this information.

If you are being offered company-sponsored financing on your housing purchase, consider it very carefully before deciding to go anywhere else. Most of these programs are very favorable to the employee, and usually the transferring company has already done the work of checking out the potential hazards in the mortgage documents.

If you are on your own regarding financing, your first decision will be the choice between fixed rate and adjustable rate. The interest rate on adjustables is usually considerably lower than that of fixed-rate mortgages. If you think, therefore, that you will be moving again within the next five or so years, an adjustable mortgage will probably be your best bet. The fixed-rate mortgage is a good choice if interest rates are in a downturn when you are house-hunting and you plan to remain in your home more or less permanently.

Snakes in the Grass

Watch out for the following little things:

Fees. The lender with the lowest advertised interest rate may not be the lender of choice. High points or exceptionally high application and processing fees can wipe out the benefits of a lower interest rate for several years. Especially if you think you will be moving again in the near future, be sure to add up all the fees before you decide which lender is offering you the best deal.

Qualifying.   Most home mortgages today are sold into the secondary mortgage market, and the qualifying guidelines are quite rigid there. You'll also be asked to prove that your down payment is cash on hand and not borrowed money. This may include producing your bank statements for several months before the date you signed the contract to buy a home.

There are some lenders, however, who are not selling their loans to Fannie Mae or Freddie Mac. You may be able to persuade these folks to stretch or bend their qualification guidelines a bit for you. During your first contact with the lender, ask if your loan will be sold into the secondary mortgage market and will therefore be subject to its guidelines, or if your lender is actually lending you the money from its own funds.

Virtually every lender will tell you during your first interview whether or not you will qualify under their guidelines for the loan you want. Processing the application is just time and paperwork. If the lender's representative says that you probably won't qualify for the loan, go elsewhere. That "probably" is almost certainly a "no" and you do not want to waste five weeks waiting for it to come through on paper.

Interest rate commitments.   With interest rates about as stable as the stock market lately, there's been a lot of fuss about how long a quoted rate should stand. No lender wants to quote a rate of, let's say, 9.5 percent for ninety days only to discover that the going rate has jumped to 10.75 percent by the end of that time period. What has happened, therefore, is the imposition of commitment choice requirements that force the borrower to share some of the risk with the lender. At most lenders today, you will be offered several mortgage commitment options from which you must make a single choice on the day you submit your mortgage application. You might choose to have your interest rate fixed for ninety days at the figure quoted on the day of your application. Or you might have it fixed at the rate that will be quoted on the day your application is approved. Or you might elect to take whatever the rate is being charged on the day of closing. (This last option is a good choice only if you think rates are going down.) Since no one can predict the future, there is some risk in each of these options. Sometimes the lender wins and sometimes the borrower wins. Choose what seems best for your particular situation.

Stipulations in the commitment. This snake has no warning rattle and it could be lethal enough to kill your purchase. To protect their own interests, some lenders are now writing into their mortgage commitments contingencies that require a contract of sale on the home the buyer is selling before the loan will be cast. The worst of these I have ever seen required that the buyer's house be sold *and* closed before the loan for the purchase of a new house would be granted.

Most sellers will not allow the sale of their house to be contingent upon the sale of the buyer's house. When such a contingency shows up in the mortgage commitment, they are often infuriated, since they consider the deal dead and their property has usually been off the market for three to six weeks because of it. Sales can and will fall through over such a clause. There is even some question as to whether it is legal for a lender to change the agreement between a buyer and seller by adding such a stipulation to the mortgage commitment. My best advice is to ask your prospective lender at the very outset if there are any contingencies regarding the sale of your current house being written into their mortgage commitments. If there are, go elsewhere.

Balloons. A balloon loan is usually a short-term deal. You take out a five- or ten-year mortgage, make payments as though it were a thirty- or forty-year mortgage, and then pay the balance of the principal at the end of its term. Of course, at that point, you still owe almost all that you borrowed.

Balloons are dangerous because they depend upon the state of things in the future. If there is a shutdown in the mortgage market similar to that of 1976 at the time your five-year note comes due and payable, what will you do? Many, but not all, lenders will write in refinancing, or roll-over, provisions in their balloon mortgages. Try to get this clause written in if an appealing balloon is offered to you.

If you know that you will be moving again in three years, however, and a low-rate five-year balloon is being offered, consider it. Your payments will probably be lower than you would be able to arrange through any other financing and your interest will be tax deductible.

The call. The call is not being used much anymore, but when it is written into a fixed-rate loan, you may be taking a viper into your home. To call a mortgage means to demand payment in full. A mortgage with the right to call written into it will allow the lender to demand full payment (or refinancing) on certain named dates in the mortgage agreement. If prevailing interest rates are higher than the rate you are paying on any of those dates, you can pretty much expect that the lender will call. Rather than take on so chancy a situation, you would do well to reconsider an adjustable-rate mortgage that is protected by caps.

Your Closing

You will need to bring a certified check for the amount of cash that you owe. Generally, it's a good idea to have this check made out to yourself. You can always endorse it over to the closing agent, but if some last-minute snag holds up the closing, you won't be stuck with a check that you can't readily turn back into cash.

Now I know this next piece of advice is going to sound tedious, but trust me and listen. When you go to your closing, take a pocket calculator with you and go through all the numbers on the closing statement. I have personally been involved in several dozen real estate closings, and I have picked up errors that the lenders, the lawyers, and the sellers have made that have amounted to thousands of dollars. Remember, human beings and/or computers are filling in the blanks. Both are capable of producing inaccurate information!

CHAPTER 11

Dual-Career Considerations

MARY STANFORD remembers that she was browning meat-balls for spaghetti on what she now calls "the night." Tom came in and stood in the doorway a second or so too long. Right then she knew something was up.

"Ta-dum!" he announced, doing a little two-step that brought him into the kitchen. "Well, my dear, it looks like Orlando."

"Orlando!" Mary hadn't meant to shriek, but it came out that way. "Or-*land*-o," she repeated more quietly but with proper emphasis. "Are you telling me you've got a job in Orlando? Are you out of your mind? Remember me? Mary Stanford, associate professor of baroque music. And you want to go to Orlando? Good God, Tom! Half the people in that city probably think Bach is a hotshot photographer who wrote a book and the other half would probably spell his name with an '*o-k*.' What will *I* do for a job? Will I have anyone to talk with? And what about the children? Where will they go to school? Cinderella's castle, maybe?

"There's no way I'm going to move to that cultural wasteland! I don't care what your title will be. I don't care how much money you'll make. I'm *not* going. Do you hear me? Not this time. No

120

way! You can go yourself if you want it so much. That's it! Why don't you just commute the thousand miles to Orlando! What the hell, airfare is cheap."

"Hold it, hold it," pleaded Tom. "I was only kidding. Joke, Mary, just a joke. I was trying to get a rise out of you. I guess I touched a little deeper than I thought."

Mary was close to tears. "That's not funny, Tom," she replied. "The thought of moving to a castle in the middle of a swamp is not funny."

Three months later, Tom Stanford's name appeared on a list of management staff cuts. He would get one year's severance pay. It took him almost half that year to find another job.

When he did, however, it was in Boston, where Mary had little trouble finding a teaching position. Life was good then. But during the turmoil of the jobless months, Mary often wondered if there had really been a job opening in Orlando. Should she have been more positive in her reaction to Tom's little feeler? Or at least more open to the possibilities of the move before saying no so inflexibly? She knew nothing about Orlando, really. Except the glimpses she had gotten on the drive between the airport and Disney World two years ago. Oh, and the crime statistics she had read in *Newsweek*. But she could find statistics just about as bad for Chicago, or New York, or even for Boston.

Mary had responded to a mental image built upon a few scraps of knowledge. If this job in Boston hadn't come up . . . well, Tom's turning down the job in Orlando would have been a disaster. "If there had been a job," she thought. Mary never did get up the courage to ask that question, and her husband never did tell her.

Tom had, in fact, been offered a position in Orlando. Not a promotion, but a secure position in a time of company cutbacks. He had refused it after seeing Mary's response. Knowing how much she loved her work, he could not deprive her of it, even at the risk of his security in the company.

This story is real. I've changed the names and particulars to protect the identities of these two people, but they could be one of any number of couples in today's two-career society. More than 50 percent of American women are now employed outside the home, and that percentage is rising every year. Decisions about a new job can no longer be made in the boss's office.

Trailing Spouses

Twenty-five years ago, no one thought much about "trailing spouses." When the husband (almost invariably the primary bread-winner) had to move for a better or perhaps a new job, the wife and kids quite naturally followed. It was what you did.

Today, over 60 percent of corporate transfers involve two-career couples. An estimate by Merrill Lynch Relocation Management, Inc., America's largest relocation firm, predicts that that number will be 75 percent by 1990. And not only are more women working outside the home, but more of them are in professional careers, where their income is equal to or greater than their husband's.

"Well, yes, that's theoretically possible," you say. "But, really now, we *are* talking about a small number here."

Perhaps, but you may be as surprised as I was to learn that the *husband* is the trailing spouse in approximately 15 percent of the corporate transfers that involve dual careers.

Handling dual-career considerations is fast becoming a major concern of employers and relocation companies alike. The problems are significant, demanding, and sometimes insoluble. Studies have shown that somewhere between 25 and 50 percent of transfer refusals are due specifically to the threat to a spouse's career.

So what to do if the question comes up for you? One professor of religion at a prestigious Massachusetts college continued in his tenured position when his wife was offered a job singing with a European opera company. They see each other over the Christmas holidays and during the summer. A woman in northwestern New Jersey refused to follow her newly promoted husband to Washington, D.C., because she did not want to leave the goats and geese she had been raising for years. He now commutes weekends.

"Fine for them," you say, "but we *like* being together. There's no question that money and professional status are important in our lives, but not important enough to get us to split up our home. You haven't talked about how these people *feel*. Is it worth it?"

You've hit the nail on the head. The questions that come up in a dual-career family bridge the "Money" and "Feelings" sections of this book. And there are few pat answers on either side.

The Problems

INCOME

When both partners in a relationship work outside the home, a relocation usually means that one of them will give up a job. This can mean household income cut by half!

Then what do you do about applying for a mortgage in your new location? How can the spouse's nonincome be taken into account? Will you have to settle for less living space? Some couples rent for a period of time, usually until the trailing spouse finds appropriate employment that will enable them to qualify for the financing they need to buy the kind of home they want. Others allow one member of the couple to move ahead. The spouse stays behind, working but also making frequent job-hunting trips to the new location. The relocation is not completed until both partners have satisfactory employment.

Still other couples search out lenders who will be flexible. This is difficult in this age when Fannie Mae and Freddie Mac, the giants of the secondary mortgage market, dominate the home-financing marketplace and dictate its rules of mortgage qualification. But there *are* lending programs available. For example, GMAC Mortgage Corporation (a subsidiary of General Motors Acceptance Corporation) will consider the trailing spouse's income in qualifying a couple for a mortgage loan if he or she has worked for the previous six months and signs a statement saying that he or she intends to find work as soon as possible. Some smaller independent lenders will also make an exception for a financially dependable couple, especially if the lender is in search of new customers or if the transferee's employer exerts a little friendly pressure. Finding a lender that will bend its qualification guidelines, however, is usually time-consuming work. And it is work that you must do yourself.

FEELINGS

In the majority of situations, it is still the husband who is transferred and the wife who must give up her job or her position in the community to follow him. Immediately after the move, the husband goes off to work at his new job. He is usually pressured by new demands upon his skills and by the task of reorienting himself both to his new position in the company and to the new physical plant and its operating procedures. More often than not, he has less time for his wife and family, and he comes home more tired than he used to. He does, however, maintain his professional status (which does no harm to his self-image) and he interacts each workday with co-workers, some of whom he probably knew, at least as telephone personalities, before the transfer.

A man who is moving without employer support, either changing jobs or starting a business of his own, faces the effort of reestablishing his professional credentials and his personal interactions with co-workers. In this case, he comes closer to the problems faced by women who follow their husbands' transfers.

With a relocation, a wife who does not work outside the home is totally cut off from her support systems. There is often a loss of identity and sometimes a diminution of self-image. Women who have made a career of active participation in their communities and in volunteer work do not carry the established respect for their skills with them to their new communities. Such a woman must essentially start over.

In addition, women with children still face the bulk of the responsibility for helping those children to find *their* place in the new community. And the task of transforming a new living space into a home does fall more heavily upon women than upon men. Some psychologists and relocation authorities even suggest that female trailing spouses delay reentry into the employment marketplace for six months or a year, or until the couple or family has worked through its relocation adjustment. Not all of us have the financial freedom to follow this advice, however, and some women prefer working outside the home to housework.

Statistically, studies show that the most problematic relocations are those in which one spouse gives up his or her career for the other, unless new and comparable employment is found. Next on the list is the relocation of the employee with a spouse who does not work in the traditional employment marketplace. The most common complaints of these spouses are feelings of isolation, disorientation, and loss of identity, and an inability to adapt to the lifestyle and cultural concerns that prevail in the new location.

LICENSES AND CERTIFICATIONS

Professional trailing spouses come up against the licensing problem when they cross state lines. Many careers require that state-administered tests be taken; others, like teaching, may require that specific college-level courses such as state history be completed before certification. In some professions, there is licensing reciprocity among neighboring states. For licensed professionals from greater distances, some states modify their licensing requirements. Real estate agents, for example, often need take only the state law part of the licensing examination and are exempt from the classroom work required before a license can be issued to a new applicant.

Your national trade or professional organization is probably your best source for information about transferring your license or certification. Be sure to allow adequate time for this chore, however, and check on the procedures in your new state as soon as you know you will be going there. Some examinations are administered only on specific dates, sometimes as seldom as twice a year!

SELF-EMPLOYMENT

You've spent seven years establishing your Irish boutique, and business has never been better. Then your husband is named VP and plant manager for a brand-new facility—in San Diego. You're sure that smiling Irish eyes will be fewer there, probably too few to support a similar boutique.

Well, perhaps you'll start a craft and gift shop. After all, your retailing experience and the skills you've developed don't even need to be packed in order to travel. Meanwhile, what can be done about the Blarney Store?

If you can get out of your lease, you can hold a magnificent going-out-of-business sale and use the cash it raises to start your new business, whatever it might be. But commercial leases are much harder to break without penalty than residential leases. If you can't easily get out of yours, you might consider putting the business only up for sale.

Although not strictly speaking a real estate transaction, businesses are sometimes listed with a local real estate broker who is a member of the local multiple listing service. Most areas also have several business brokers who specialize in finding commercial buyers who will pay for the stock and the established trade and take over an existing lease. They charge either a flat fee or a commission. Before you hunt down one of these business brokers, however, check with your landlord to be sure he will accept a new tenant in your place.

"Good advice," you say. "But I own the building."

Okay. Try marketing your business and your building separately. If someone wants to buy both, all the better, but you might be able to sell only the business more readily. Set the rent to be charged the new business owner high enough to cover the building's carrying expenses. Such an arrangement could turn out to be a very good investment if you are located in an economically healthy area. Be sure, however, that you see your attorney about arranging a lease with the new business owner. There are several kinds of commercial leases. For long-distance ownership situations, the triple net lease in which the tenant pays all utility and maintenance fees is often a good choice.

If you are not interested in keeping tabs on investment property halfway across the country, you can list your building for sale even though you have sold the business within it. Your tenant will want an ironbound lease for several years, but commercial property often takes that long to sell.

Some types of self-employment relocate more easily, especially those that are home-based. As a writer, I simply pack up my files and my word processor and go. No trauma. My connections are as secure as the nation's telephone network.

Relocation as a real estate investor is somewhat more bothersome because investors often choose to sell properties and reinvest close to their new home. But this need not be the case. Reliable property managers can be hired, and your investment real estate can continue to show positive cash flow and appreciation. Keeping your vacation home as investment property can bring in a nice income and provide you with a chance to spend a few weeks a year back in your old hometown.

Employer Assistance

Because it is usually easier and more cost-effective to transfer an employee who has proven himself or herself capable and competent than to train a new person, many companies are responding to employee resistance to transfer by offering help with spouse reemployment. In some cases, relocation firms are establishing separate spouse employment counseling centers. Many of these centers pledge to stay with the trailing spouse until he or she finds a satisfactory and satisfying job.

Job assistance programs often include extensive career aptitude testing, the kind that can cost hundreds of dollars if you were to seek it privately. Such testing can lead you to a new profession or help you to explore new aspects of your old one. Also included in most spouse assistance programs are résumé preparation, cover letter preparation, interviewing techniques, and even referrals to the "right" people in the "right" places.

On a more informal basis, some employers try to find jobs for spouses within their company. But, of course, this isn't always possible. Procter & Gamble, for example, would hardly have a job for an astrophysicist. As a result, networking groups have been born. Over lunch, personnel directors and relocation specialists from several area companies get together and talk about employment possibilities for spouses of newly transferred employees. As you might guess, a good deal of trading goes on.

Helping Yourself

No matter how much relocation counseling is promised to you, landing a job in your new location is something you must do for yourself. Whether you want to have the job secured before you leave your old location, job-hunt immediately upon arrival in your new area, or delay your reemployment until after you and your family are adjusted to your new environment, at some point *you* will have to go out into the marketplace and apply for work. And this includes volunteer work if that is your career choice. Facing this task means facing the possibility of rejection. Try not to take turndowns personally, especially at this time when your new rooting in the area is still tenuous.

There are many good career advice and job-hunting books available today. Try your local library. If you don't see anything on their shelves that satisfies you, ask the reference librarian to allow you to look through the current *Subject Guide to Books in Print.* Check under "Employment," "Career Guidance," or "Jobs" until you come up with a list of promising titles. Books that are currently in print can be ordered through a local bookstore.

Most people who have had to change jobs several times will tell you that the real "in" to most employers comes from personal referrals rather than résumés submitted to personnel departments. If you are not getting help from an employer assistance program, have your spouse ask among his co-workers about the jobs their spouses have. If something sounds promising, make an effort to get together socially with this co-worker and his or her spouse. Also ask your neighbors about where they work and what they do. As you become a part of local social groups (including newcomers' clubs), community action or recreation groups, or religious groups, ask their members about employment opportunities. In fact, tell everyone whom you trust that you are looking for a job. And, of course, check out the local employment agencies. These range in specialty from temporary help placement to CEO headhunters.

PART II

Feelings

CHAPTER 12

Moving Means Change

FOR A MOMENT, if you will, try to imagine me knee-deep in scholarly publications containing articles written by psychologists and associate professors, trade magazines devoted to relocation in all its aspects, directories, oversized and very dry books, and bulging files marked "Moving" that are filled with magazine and newspaper clippings dating back as far as 1981. From this pond of paper, two ideas emerge again and again: *moving is like dealing with death* and *moving is like dealing with divorce*. Pretty awful, huh?

"Oh, come on!" you say. "It can't be that bad. What about the move that involves a promotion with a destination that everyone is looking forward to? Or how about the move thirty miles west to a much nicer house, let's say a house with lake frontage? Surely, you can't compare that kind of move to death or divorce!"

It's not me, folks! Just about all the psychologists who have studied the problem agree on this one. In one way or another, they come to the conclusion that moving brings about a sense of loss even when the move is much desired and a matter of choice.

My own experience in our seven moves verifies their findings, as does the many hours I've spent over coffee both with newcomers

and with soon-to-be-transferred friends in the highly mobile corporate ghetto where we live. There's no doubt about it: *moving means
change and change means loss.*

Identifying the Losses

YOUR NICHE

Most obviously, moving means loss of your geographical niche in
the world. One of our moves was literally up the hill, about a mile
and a half total distance. My husband and I thought there would
certainly be no moving trauma in this one. The children didn't
even change schools. But we were about to be surprised.

Not long after we moved into our new house, we began to realize
how much the children's day-to-day recreational world is bounded
by how far you can walk or ride your bike. The change of neighborhood cut off their ready access to established playmates. They could
no longer just go outdoors and find someone familiar. Get-togethers
had to be arranged and one parent or the other had to drive. "I have
no one to play with" became an annoying refrain in our lives.

Even more surprising was the sense of loss that I experienced
with this short move. I found myself going to a different corner
store for milk, to a different bakery, and to a different dry cleaner.
When I stopped back at one of the "old" places one day, I felt
separated. I was no longer really a part of that neighborhood.

I'm sure you're thinking that these are rather minor problems.
And I agree. But that was a particularly short move and therefore
also a small loss. The greater the distance of a relocation, the
greater the geographic disorientation, which means the greater the
change and therefore the greater the loss.

Think about the last time you rearranged the furniture in your
bedroom. Isn't it true that for a while you were disoriented? Especially in the night. Now assign a number to your degree of disorientation over the furniture change and multiply it by an exponent

that will produce so many new numbers that you'll lose track of where to put the commas. That's what moving means in terms of geographic disorientation.

The greater the distance you move, the higher the exponent. A long-distance relocation means adjusting not only to a new corner store but also to changes in climate, terrain, and even customs. Loss of your geographic niche means that the car won't drive itself home anymore and you may not have the white Christmases you have been accustomed to since childhood.

YOUR STATUS

Even though people employed outside the home maintain status in and through their jobs, a move of more than fifty miles usually means some loss of community status. It will be some time before you are recognized in your new community as the exceptionally fine Little League coach you are. It will be some time before the choir director in your new church recognizes your spouse's potential for solos. Your daughter will have to prove again what an excellent stage manager she is. And your son will have to earn again that place on the varsity that he had worked so hard to achieve in his old school.

The loss of community status often is accompanied by some loss of self-esteem and sometimes even with some loss of self-identity. This is especially true among teens, for whom peer acceptance is so important and group membership is a significant factor in one's sense of identity.

Among adults, career identity acts as a buffer to loss of self-esteem, allowing for community status to be rebuilt gradually. Homemakers, however, sometimes feel the loss of identity even more than do teens. There is no group outside the home to which they automatically belong (like it or not). There is no place to which they must go each day to interact with the people that are there. All connections with the community, status, and even identity must be rebuilt through self-motivated efforts.

Your Support System

I had always been annoyed by women in the supermarket who meet at the end of an aisle and stop to chat about how Suzy and Sammy are doing in their respective colleges. Everyone else in the store has to work around these two happily chattering people and gridlock becomes a distinct possibility. Then we relocated and I felt envy rather than annoyance. For months, I had not met anyone in the supermarket who smiled and said hello, much less asked about how my particular version of Suzy was doing.

Acquaintances, members of your social group, and tried-and-true friends are the casualties of a long-distance relocation. They are the support system you have become accustomed to and will now have to rebuild from scratch. For people moving away from nearby family members, the loss is even greater.

Now, I do understand that these losses are not nearly as devastating or permanent as the loss one feels in connection with a death. And they are not as emotionally painful and life-changing as a divorce. But they are losses. You will not often see the people of a particular support system, and you will never again interact with them in the same relationship that you shared as neighbors.

Responding to the Threat of Loss

We begin responding to a relocation not when it occurs, but when we realize that it will occur. Once we know there will be a change, we react to the threat of loss. During the past ten years, many studies have found that most people go through similar stages of experience in dealing with loss or the threat of loss, no matter what motivates the loss. Some people, however, stay longer and feel more intensely in one stage than in others.

DISBELIEF OR DENIAL

"We're not really going." "This isn't really happening to me!" Many people go through a period of time when they *say* they understand and accept the fact that they will soon be moving out of the area, but intuitively they feel that the news is not real. Some time in the future, yes. But not now. "I'll think about it tomorrow" is a common thought pattern at this stage.

The most common manifestation of denial is the refusal to take any action that is involved with the move. Some people don't seek information about the new area. Some won't begin to take the steps of physical and emotional uncoupling that are necessary to leave their old area. And some talk about what they're going to do and how they're going to do it, but do nothing.

Roger and Carmen are a good example of a couple who stayed in the denial stage much too long. The magnificent new house they were having custom-built sixty miles from their present house was nearly finished when the builder called and notified them that he would like to close in thirty days. At that point, the couple had not yet taken any steps to get their present home ready for sale.

The truth of the matter was that Carmen did not want to move, no matter how wonderful the house was. She had become so much a part of the community where they had lived for thirteen years. Roger said he was looking forward to the move, especially since it would change his commute to work from seventy minutes to ten minutes, but he somehow just never got around to putting the house on the market.

This couple moved into their new house in time for their daughter to start school in the new town. Their old house stood vacant for seven months before an offer to buy came in. Seven months of making payments on two mortgages!

If Roger and Carmen had acted rationally rather than emotionally in response to their move, they would have put their old home on the market during the eight months that it took to get their new home built. Yet, if you talked with either of them during the building period, each would tell you how exciting the process of having a house custom-built was, and how much they each looked forward to the move. Only their lack of action revealed their denial.

DEPRESSION OR JUST PLAIN SADNESS

"Feeling down. Feeling blue. Just can't seem to get motivated. Don't really care about anything." These are ways people describe their responses to grief. It is unfashionable in our society to say, "I feel sad," so we waltz around the emotion. If we could admit it, most of us would feel better.

Common manifestations of depression are lack of appetite or compulsive eating (whichever your particular body type dictates), lack of motivation, claiming, "I don't care," and inability to meet commitments.

A teenage boy I know refused to compete in a wrestling tournament in which he had an excellent chance to win. "It doesn't matter to me," he said. In walking away, he let his teammates down. His parents and I both thought that he just couldn't handle the sadness he felt at leaving, and therefore acted in a way that would cause resentment among the people he most cared about and begin the process of separation that he could not consciously face.

ANGER

You can't be angry at moving in the way you can be angry at the drunk driver who smashes into the rear of your car. Until it is actually happening, moving is a concept, something that will happen in the future. Its intangibility makes it a poor target for anger.

So what do we do with the anger we feel at the thought of all the losses the move will entail? We displace it.

Real estate agents report that long-distance house-hunters on their first trips are often difficult to deal with. They find fault with everything, make disparaging comments, and are generally unpleasant. Often husband and wife argue over insignificant details. "Was there a linen closet in the bathroom?" is a good example. It goes:

"Was there a linen closet in the bathroom of that house?"

"How the hell do I know!"

"Well, you always want your towels stored in the bathroom. We can't possibly buy a house with the linen closet in the hallway. I'm just not going to listen to you bitch about no towels every morning!"

"You can't be serious. I love that house. So what if the linen closet is in the hallway! You just don't want to take on any of the responsibility for keeping towels in the bathroom. Maybe that's too much for you, dear."

And so on. Woe to the real estate agent who might suggest that a linen closet be built into the bathroom. These prospective buyers are not arguing about a linen closet. They are just angry at the realization that everything will not be the same as it is in the home to which they are now accustomed.

Families with teenagers know a lot about displaced anger. I've seen teens start playing hard rock on a stereo at a sound level that shakes the house every time a real estate agent starts a showing. Or perhaps they'll dye their hair fuchsia and mat it together with hair dressing so that it looks like porcupine quills and then come to the dinner table as though nothing has happened. The teen is just looking for a fight with his or her parents, a fight that will allow some of the anger to be vented.

Anger and depression sometimes continue long after the actual physical move has taken place. In fact, many psychologists and relocation counselors believe that it takes from six months to two years in the new location to dispel all the negative emotions involved in a relocation.

TRADEOFFS AND COMPROMISES

Try telling the skier from Utah that he'll love living in Jacksonville, Florida. Encouragement like "After all, John, you can play golf just about twelve months a year" won't make him feel any better. Or try telling the opera fan from New York City that there's good theater in Dallas.

Moving a considerable distance is bound to mean giving up some of the special interests inherent in a particular place. These cannot be replaced and are a loss that must be mourned. But when a person can recognize that the new location has some special offerings of its own and can take an interest in them, the beginning of a positive attitude has started. It can happen when the skier discovers that there's first-rate white-water rafting within a day's drive or when the opera fan discovers that he can sing in the local theater group production of *Carousel*.

ACCEPTANCE

You'll know when you and each of the members of your family get to this stage. Your daughter might call from school and say, "Mom, can I bring Sarah home with me today? Just for a little while, please!" Or you might drop onto the couch exhausted from painting those blasted six-panel doors and see a deer standing in your backyard. "Hello, how nice that we'll be neighbors," you think.

Your memories of your old home will still be a part of your life, but that life will be going forward. And the place you are now living will be home.

How to Make It Easier

Recognition is the key. Understand and accept that you will feel the feelings associated with change. Change always means there will be some loss. Work through your losses, mourn them if necessary, but don't deny them.

Looking forward is also a help to many families. Look for positives. New vacation places, new activities. For some, it helps to focus on the idea of a new start. Leaving behind old hang-ups and sometimes old pain. For others, it helps to think of working together as a team to make the move work. Many families are actually brought closer by a relocation.

Most of all, try to be open to new ideas, new people, new ways of doing things. The way you do things now may be perfect, nothing could be better, you might say to yourself, but perhaps some other way, in some other place, with some other people might be just as perfect.

CHAPTER 13

Uprooting

RELOCATING A PERSON is a little like transplanting an evergreen tree. No matter how huge a ball of earth you wrap in burlap, some roots are broken to be left in the ground. Breaking those roots is absolutely necessary to the move, yet it must be painful, even to a tree. A new system of roots will grow in the new location, however, and the tree will be stronger and grow more quickly for having been transplanted. So, too, with humans.

The process and the pain of breaking ties and getting oneself balled and burlaped differs with the age, life stage, and lifestyle of the person to be transplanted. Let's look at some examples.

Toddlers to Prekindergarten

The family is the world of the two-and-a-half-year-old to four-year-old. Moving has little effect in terms of coping with the environment. But these very young children do become anxious about change within the family or within their living area. Quite naturally, the absence of parents during house-hunting trips is stressful.

Even when parents are at home, however, the preschooler often senses that something is different in the household and perhaps catches (unverbalized) a little of the anxiety and uncertainty that parents may be feeling.

While working as a real estate agent, I observed yet another source of anxiety that has been overlooked by all of the children's books about moving day. Many children are frightened by the changes that occur when a home is listed for sale. They do not understand what is happening. Why do toys have to be picked up and put away at the ring of the telephone? Who are these people walking about the house, opening closets, and turning lights on and off?

Children old enough to understand that the house is for sale and that a move is imminent are often impatient with the process. Sometimes they sense their parents' worry if the house does not sell quickly. You may hear them ask, "Who will buy our house?" But that question may also mean *Who will want it?* or *Why doesn't anyone want it?*

The workings of the real estate marketplace are far beyond the comprehensive abilities of this age level. If your child seems worried about selling the house, explain simply that every house must wait until someone who is just right for it comes along. Explain that there's nothing wrong with your house, but that not every house is right for every person. It might help to use animal images to help the child visualize this idea. A bear sleeps in a cave, a horse in a stable, a rabbit in a hole. Different people also have different housing needs.

Toys are another problem in selling a house with young children. What the child considers most precious is often left lying about as though it were of no concern. Kevin, a four-year-old, was crazy about building blocks. On one occasion, he had built a whole city on the floor of his room. Then, while he was out shopping with his mother, a real estate agent showed his house to a family who had their children in tow. The agent and the parents thoughtlessly told the children to play in the little boy's room while they looked about. Needless to say, the children disassembled the entire city. Kevin came home to devastation. He cried and carried on and declared that he hated all house-buyers and that he hoped that nobody would ever buy the house.

Regrettably, such incidents are not uncommon. To avoid them, be sure that you or your children put away all that is precious to them whenever you leave the house. Leave signs that say DO NOT TOUCH on the prized items that cannot be put out of sight.

When the parents of a preschooler have divorced and the relocation will move the child some distance from one of them, there can be some emotional problems. Sometimes the parent to be left behind burdens the child unnecessarily by verbalizing how much he or she will miss his or her baby. The child sees the parent's distress and feels that somehow he is causing it.

If you are in such a divorce situation, realize that the separation itself will be stressful to your child. Do not intensify the anxiety and sadness your child is feeling by adding your own feelings to the myriad of emotions he or she is working through. Try to emphasize the positives: the fact that you, the parent being left behind, will stay in the area, and when the child visits you, he or she can also visit old friends and favorite places. If possible, promise to visit the child at least once in the new location. It is important for the young child to realize that distances can be traveled, and that the parent being left behind will not just drop out of his or her life.

Even when divorce is not a factor in a relocation, it is important to reassure the preschool child that moving will not mean separation from parents and siblings. Tell him or her that the whole family, all the pets, and all the toys will be moving, and that you will all live together in a new house. What you are really trying to tell your child is: Your world will not be changed by this move.

Five- to Twelve-Year-Olds

Most child-raising books are in agreement that this is the easiest age to move children. Even though school friends and activities are more important now, the family is still the center of their lives. During this life stage, the child is likely to reflect the attitudes of his or her parents. If the parents are anxious, the child will be anxious. If the parents are positive about the move, the child will probably be positive, too.

All that I said about divorce in the previous section about pre-schoolers applies to this age group also. You may choose to change the words you use, but the message you convey to your child should be the same.

One of the concerns often expressed by parents who plan a move is when to do it. Should they move in the middle of a school year or wait until June?

For the elementary school child—in fact, even for the middle school child—there are pros and cons here. I tend to favor moving during the course of the school year. During this time, your child is introduced into his class as a new student and given an orientation tour of the school. Because the child is the new person in a group of known people, most teachers take a little more care in placing him or her properly in math and reading groups. The child, meanwhile, has an opportunity to make some acquaintances before the long summer vacation.

Incorrect placement, especially in a middle school, can be very stressful to the student and complicate the process of settling in. Sometimes it can be disastrous. One family moving from North Carolina to California chose a particular location because it had a good school system. They moved in late August, however, and records were late in arriving at the new school. That school's staff assumed that any child moving into their community would be behind their students at any given grade level. They assigned the fourteen-year-old daughter of the family to slow-moving English and math classes.

The child immediately expressed her unhappiness with the school, but her parents assumed she was just going through a post-moving depression. They did not discover the problem with the academic placement until late October. By then, the school refused to alter her placement and her schedule because it would be "disruptive."

How bad was the placement? The girl was accepted at an Ivy League college from her junior year of high school. But that achievement cost the parents five years of private school tuition. The moral of this story: Be certain there is plenty of time for your child's records to arrive (hand-carry them if you can) and have as many standardized test results with you as you can get when you enroll your child in a new school. Then be sure to observe closely what your child is studying and how he or she is responding to classwork, teachers, and fellow students.

Teens

Teens seem to do better if they are allowed to finish out the year in their old school and start at a new school in the fall. In a mid-year change, there are often problems with courses that are different or simply not offered. Leaving is also more difficult for the high school student because athletes do not want to desert their teams, musicians their groups, and club members their offices and responsibilities.

American high school students also tend to form tight cliques. These are almost impossible to break into once the year is under way. In the fall, however, the clique structure is weakest and most open to new members. Even where to sit in the lunchroom has not yet been determined.

Teens find moving more painful than any other age group. This is the time when they are forming an identity apart from their family. The teen peer group helps the teen to make this sometimes painful but very necessary separation. A relocation requires that the ties to the group be broken. The teenager is thrown back upon the family as his or her only support system.

Some teens are so rebellious and resentful on hearing of their imminent relocation that they actually try to sabotage moving plans. They refuse to keep their rooms clean, they bad-mouth the house, the town, and the schools to prospective buyers and real estate agents, and they throw temper tantrums that might end up with fists through a door or dents in the walls. Many parents of high school seniors give in and arrange for their son or daughter to live with friends or relatives in order to finish out that last year with established friends.

Teens simply have not had enough experience to understand that change and adapting to change are continuing parts of the life process. They don't seem to remember life before high school and can't visualize life after it. If you can, try to talk with your teenager about the fact that the relocation could be a fine preparation for college or entering the job market. It's an opportunity to test one's ability to survive in a new environment and to try out social skills with a clean slate.

Your teen may tearfully nod and agree with all that you say about opportunity and growth, yet still mourn the coming separation. He or she will not believe you if you add that teenage friendships rarely survive a move by more than six months. Nor will the teen believe that in six months new friends may be more important in his or her life than the friends that will be left behind. Your son or daughter will think that you *just don't understand!*

"That stuff about new friends may be true for the average kid. But I'm different. I'm much more loyal and deep-feeling than most kids my age," your teen will probably think. And then, almost inevitably, your almost-grown child will wonder why his or her own parent can't appreciate depth of character and loyalty in one's own offspring. So don't spend too much time talking with teens about the logistics of friendship. Some things in life one must discover for oneself.

A special relocation problem is the teenage romance. Teens in love are certain that it's forever. You, therefore, are the villain who is moving them apart. It's not a pleasant role to play. If the distance is not too great, promise frequent visits. If the relocation will be distant and permanent, some professional counseling may be necessary to help your teen, and in fact the whole family, through the trauma. One of the most psychologically devastating positions is the feeling of having no choice. And that is exactly where the relocating teen is when he or she must move and leave behind a loved one.

Parents and Couples Without Children

Although moving with children usually means taking on their problems with your own, there are occasional bright spots. Often some of your friends are the parents of your children's friends. This is the best of all possible worlds, since visits can be planned back and forth to the satisfaction of all. Saying good-bye then is close to saying, "See you again soon."

But for couples without children, or parents who have friends not connected with their children (and who doesn't?), there are some good-byes that must simply be good-byes. Mourn the loss, but don't let it rule your life.

Divorced Parents

A divorced parent moving out of an area often has a difficult time uprooting since the move means leaving the children behind. As I have said, it is most important not to burden your child with the knowledge of the pain you are feeling upon separation. Acknowledge that you will miss the child but try to talk about the visits you will have in the future.

In your own mind, try to think of the relocation as a chance for a fresh start. Remind yourself that the relationship to your child is not tied to place. It may even turn out to be refreshing to interact with your child in your new area, a place that doesn't have memories.

Singles

Singles without romantic ties are the most mobile sector of our population. Sometimes they may feel a bit of homesickness if the relocation is their first move away from family and hometown. But singles also have the most mobility and opportunities for return visits.

Saying Good-bye

As relocation becomes imminent, people seem to choose one of two attitudes toward their current community. Either they idealize it: *We'll never find another place as nice as this*. Or they begin to focus in on its every fault: *Can't stand the traffic, taxes are too high, weather stinks*, etc., etc. A few people actually vacillate between these two camps.

Try not to get yourself too deeply into either. Both are emotionally based responses and usually distortions of reality. Recognize that people do have a tendency to have such feelings and then try to keep *your* attitudes rational.

To say good-bye, visit favorite places and people one last time before you leave. Take pictures. Have a farewell dinner with your closest friends. Do whatever it takes to mark the event of leaving as special. Don't dwell on final, however. Your farewell dinner is not a funeral gathering. Think and say, "We can come back. We'll visit again." The words ring with reassurance.

CHAPTER 14

Settling In

YOU'RE GOING to feel lonely. Count on it. Even if your work in the new location brings you into contact with hundreds of people a day, you're going to feel lonely. Certainly, one of the major losses in a relocation is the loss of friends.

After you relocate, you will go through a period of time when you seem to be meeting new people everywhere, every day. From these introductions, you will begin to build a group of acquaintances, some of whom you'll know only in their occupational roles—the women at the library desk, for example—and others who will become a part of your social group, people you meet again and again at cocktail parties or perhaps people you regularly play bridge with. You will be able to build a network of acquaintances in your new community quite quickly if you make an effort to do so. But friends take time and shared experiences.

People who don't mind working alone, who make decisions independently, and who will go to the movies or to a gathering without a partner tend to adjust more quickly to a relocation. Those who see group membership as a part of their identity (especially teens) tend to take somewhat longer. But the process of making friends is about the same for both groups. The person who knows everyone who is anyone in town after six months does not necessarily have more friends than the person who is still using a map to get around.

Some people who relocate frequently simply don't try to make the kind of friends that one would confide secrets to. They get involved in community activities and accept the jobs they do well, they volunteer for responsible roles in religious or social groups, and they attend group functions. After not very long in the community, they are often invited to parties and other private social gatherings. Their days are full, and they have a network of people whom they can call for help or just a chat, but they don't have close friends. To some degree, this is a self-preservation technique that avoids the agony of breaking close ties at every transfer.

A British fourteen-year-old who had already lived on five continents told me quite glibly that she had no friends. There was never time enough to make friends, she said. But she assured me that she had lots of acquaintances all over the world and that she was busy and really quite happy. "I guess my best friend is my mother," she said. "But, you know, that's not all that bad."

Most of us, however, don't move that often and most of us do yearn for a friend or two. That's part of the settling-in process, getting to know a few people you can laugh and cry with. So where do you begin?

Finding Others in the Same Boat

NEWCOMERS' CLUBS

The standard advice to relocating people is: Join either the local Welcome Wagon or newcomers' club. There, the theory goes, you will meet other people like yourself who recently moved into the area. Within its limits, this is good advice, but you should be aware that these are primarily daytime groups (luncheons, crafts, theater, etc.) and that the daytime participants are the wives of corporate management personnel. When these groups do sponsor evening events, the attendance is just about exclusively married couples. If you don't fit this profile, you will probably have difficulty finding a comfortable place for yourself in the group. And even some people who do fit the profile don't like the membership.

I belonged to a newcomers' group for two years after one of our relocations. At the time, it was right for me. I had three young children and not a friend or relative in sight. In the group, I met other women with whom I shared common problems. We helped each other. Membership in such a group is not without commitment, however. Be aware that if you remain a member longer than your initial year, it is almost an unwritten law that you will accept an office or committee chairmanship in the group. And certainly you will find yourself hostessing luncheons or meetings in your home.

COMPANY CLUBS

Some employers transfer so many employees each year that they run their own newcomer-type clubs. Membership is usually for two years, with last year's newcomers helping this year's to get established.

MILITARY LIFE

On military bases, there is so much coming and going that practically everyone is a newcomer. Few military families who live on base actually ever attempt to become a part of the community. Their life is almost self-contained within the perimeter of the military installation, and bases around the world are surprisingly similar to each other. Readjustment after a transfer is minimal. In fact, studies show that military children have few of the adjustment problems associated with moving that most other children have. It is as though they are in the same place but with different people. And social groups for both children and adults are more open on a military base because everyone is subject to being "new" at some time or another.

New Construction

Just about anyone who has ever had a house built in a tract development or bought an apartment in a new condominium community will tell you that there's another way to make connections that isn't as often written about as the get-together clubs. When everyone moves into a building, garden apartment community, or tract housing development at more or less the same time (within a year or so of each other), there is usually a great effort made to get to know each other. Welcome parties for the newest arrivals are common and people seem to reach out to each other to help with common problems.

One example of such community interaction is the adult babysitting co-op. Nearby parents sit for each other's children, depositing hours in their "account" that they can then withdraw at a later date by using any member of the sitters' co-op. This kind of arrangement not only provides access to reliable sitters but also brings people together in each other's houses. Many friendships begin over a cup of coffee in the kitchen after the parents return home.

Forging Friendships

Adults

Friendship is a fragile thing at its inception. It starts when two people are drawn to each other and share a mutual concern, hobby, or source of pleasure or competition. When you feel such camaraderie, however, don't just expect friendship to follow. It doesn't usually happen that way.

If you genuinely like someone you have met at a get-together or a party, don't be shy about suggesting another shared experience, whether it be a golf game or a shopping outing. If you wait for the other person to ask you first, an invitation may never arrive; he or she may also be waiting for you.

If you feel uncomfortable about making a date to do something together, you might take Ben Franklin's advice and borrow something from the person. Franklin believed that the borrowing/lending situation establishes a relationship quickly, and I agree. The lender feels generous and the borrower grateful; already there is feeling between two people. Just don't forget to return whatever it is you borrowed.

Joining group activity in response to some errors of the builder, a plan of the municipality, an unfair practice in the schools, or whatever has gotten people angry is another good way to put yourself into a situation conducive to bonding. There's nothing like working together for a purpose to start the fires of friendship glowing.

VERY YOUNG CHILDREN

Friendship between two- to five-year-olds is a matter of familiarity. It is almost essential that you invite other children of this age group into your home. Do this even if a child close in age to yours lives next door. Very young children quite literally do not know how to introduce themselves. You will need to help at first by teaching them each other's names and playing games together with them.

When both parents work, a child spending five days a week in a good day-care center will eventually form some friendships with other children in the center. A quality day-care facility is usually better for the relocated child than arranged baby-sitting in the home, since the child left at home has no chance to meet other children in the area. If you want to improve the quality of your child's time in the center, invite some of the children, one at a time, to play in your home during weekends and holidays. You'll almost certainly get to know the parents in doing so. Many adult friendships get their start in exactly this way.

GRADE SCHOOL CHILDREN

At the elementary school level, there are few school-sponsored activities to support the formation of friendships, and the playground during recess is not a good place for the new child. He or she is often left out of groups and games. No one bothers with introductions and few children make any effort to talk with the newcomer. Generally speaking, children lack the social skills to make a stranger feel welcome. Usually, the new kid has to earn his way into a group by accepting challenges or doing favors. The old story of the new kid on the block is as valid today as ever.

If you move with children in the six-to-twelve age group, try to help them get interested in after-school groups such as Scouts; Little League, soccer, or other organized sports; or the 4-H clubs. Also make it a point to invite some of the children your child has met into your home for a few hours of play after school or on a Saturday. At first, invite only one child at a time so that one-to-one bonding can be assured. One "friend" made in this way can help a child to be accepted by a whole group of playground friends.

TEENS

Most teens would rather die (or live as hermits in their rooms) than have their parents obviously participate in trying to help them make friends. You might, however, point out some pathways. Many high schools have welcoming parties for newcomers at the end of August, before school starts. The best of these groups compile lists of telephone numbers and addresses for all the new students. Some of these lists even include information on where each new student is from and a few lines about hobbies, sports, and interests. When the newcomers' lists also include information on accomplishments or positions or offices held in the old school, they help the new student to bring his credentials to the new community. A line like "Played Emily in *Our Town*" can point the way to friendships with others of similar interests.

Parents of newcomer teens can volunteer to help compile, print, and distribute these lists. Be sure, however, that they are available not only to other newcomers but also to the school population in general and the faculty and coaches.

In many high schools in the United States, there are some newcomers more spotlighted than your teen is likely to be. They are foreign exchange students. American Field Service and Youth for Understanding are two of the larger exchange groups placing students in American schools, but there are many others. Virtually all schools that accept foreign exchange students also have a foreign students' club, by one name or another. The purpose of the clubs is to foster international goodwill by helping Americans to get to know representatives of other countries and by helping the exchange student to feel at home in the United States. Most clubs have parties once a month or so and many supervised activities such as apple-picking, sailing, car washes to raise funds, and field trips to local attractions.

Membership in such a club is an excellent way for the American newcomer to meet someone a little worse off in the adjustment scene (the foreign student also knows no one and often has a language barrier to boot), to extend a helping hand, and to meet other students willing to extend that same helping hand. Inviting the exchange student to share a family outing or even a dinner at your home will help to make him or her feel accepted and might lead to a friendship.

Getting to Know the Natives

If you know you'll be leaving in a year or two, you may be perfectly happy with acquaintances, and perhaps a friend or two who moved in at the same time you did and will probably be leaving at about the same time. But if your relocation is more or less permanent, you will want to get to know some of the townsfolk, and eventually to become one of them. This cannot be done by going to work each day, watching TV each evening, and mowing your lawn and pruning your shrubs each weekend. You've got to get out of the house and go into the community.

SHARED INTERESTS

Your talents can be your ticket in. Join groups that interest you. It doesn't matter what the group is or does, as long as you are genuinely interested.

One relocation "advice" article I read suggested that the newcomer buy a cute breed of dog and go to dog-training classes as a way to meet people. Now this might work well if you love dogs and are interested in obedience competition. But if you don't, following that advice would be taking on an extra burden when you are already pretty much burdened out!

If you love tennis, spend the money to join a tennis club. If you're a history buff, search out the local historical society or buildings preservation group. Or perhaps you enjoy coaching children's sports teams; they never have enough volunteers! Or you might like to take art lessons at the local night school.

Whatever it is that you like to do outside your home, go out and find it. You cannot wait for things to happen to you or for groups to find you. They won't. Make phone calls, ask questions, volunteer, read, do whatever you have to do to find other people interested in the same things you are interested in.

WORKPLACE ACQUAINTANCES

Most workplace relationships do not usually survive outside the workplace. If you want your friends at work to become your friends after work, get involved in some spare-time activities with them. Choral groups, bowling leagues, exercise groups, gourmet dining groups, bridge groups—the list can go on and on. And, then, if you want real friends from within these groups, invite them into your home. There's nothing like breaking bread together, as the Bible says, to warm up a friendship.

A LITTLE GIVING

Volunteering to help someone in trouble is another way to make lasting connections. Seven years ago, my youngest child had a massive brain tumor removed from the cerebellum area at the base of his skull. It would not be an exaggeration to say that he brushed shoulders with death. At the time, we had only recently moved into our town, but during the thirty-five days that our son was in the hospital, our neighbors provided hot meals for our table. These people, most of whom were barely acquaintances, became our friends.

And perhaps that is what becoming a part of a community is really about: sharing and giving (if you'll pardon the old clichés). It is shared emotion, donated time, and the experience of working and playing together that bonds people together.

One very shy twenty-two-year-old whom I know volunteered for the Big Brother program in the city where he got his first job. When he did this, he was three states away from the place he had called home all his life and he knew no one. Life after work was lonely. Today, nine months later, he has made connections with people of all ages through the program. In fact, he has become part of a living community.

HIGH SCHOOL NATIVES

The American high school is an exclusive institution. It's hard to get in! Not physically, of course, but socially. Psychological studies show that fourteen- to eighteen-year-olds have the most difficult time with relocation and a primary reason for the difficulty is the clique system prevalent in most schools. Newcomers are not really welcomed by the majority of the student body despite printed messages to the contrary.

Studies also show that newcomer teens usually react to the closed social group structure in one of two ways. Some teens become more extroverted and try to buy their way into high school society by having the best car or computer, doing favors, giving parties, etc. Others withdraw and wait for high school to be over.

The second approach is more common and more difficult to break out of. No one will seek out the withdrawn student, whereas the pseudo-extrovert may eventually find a group in which he or she feels comfortable. In either case, however, relocation during the high school years is a high-risk decision. Every parent worries about their teen "getting in with the wrong group." They are concerned that group membership will be chosen not because of shared interests but simply because that particular group will accept the student. This is the stuff of nightmares.

Research has also come up with the observation that the high school students who are most successful with relocation are those who participate in athletics. I think this is probably true, but not from any particular benefit of athletic participation per se. It seems to me that working together to win against a school rival, sharing both joy and disappointment, voicing gripes at the coach, participating in efforts to raise money, and the sense of identity in wearing the school uniform wipe out many of the barriers to friendship and group association. The student becomes "one of us" because he or she acts in the common cause.

I was reminded of just how instinctive this response is recently by my dogs. (I have three.) Now dogs in the wild are pack animals and work and live as a group, sometimes better than humans. When I agreed to care for a friend's dog while she was on vacation, I did not expect the rejection that took place in my house. My three growled and barked, the hair on their backs standing straight up every time Puccini came within ten feet of any one of them.

This went on for a day and a half until one of my dogs happened to see the golden retriever from down the street walking about in our backyard. My three *and* Puccini ran to the sliding glass door, barking and jumping at the intruder.

From that moment on, Puccini belonged. There was not another growl in the house. In fact, he sometimes ate from the same bowl as the others.

If you believe that instincts are a part of human personality, as I do, you could say that there is a group survival instinct among teens. You could then even go further and say that the way to break it down is to act with the group against something outside the group.

But what do you do if your teen hates anything that involves taking one breath more than necessary, has two left feet, or simply refuses to join in athletic competition? Try to get him or her interested in some school activity where the students work together for a common cause. It takes no dramatic talent to be a stagehand for the school play, but friendships are formed backstage while the rehearsals go on. If your student does have a dramatic, musical, or writing talent, work in the school chorus, on the newspaper, or in a play will serve exactly the same function as going out for the football team. Your student will no longer be the kid from somewhere else but rather a working member of the school community.

Time

None of the goals of settling in can be accomplished in the first week you are in your new home. Making acquaintances takes time, becoming a member of a group takes time, making friends takes time. If you feel lonely, or your teen feels lonely, make a bowl of buttered popcorn and talk about old times and the friends left behind. Call back and say hello if you like. Then look forward. Try to plan something that will be fun. Invite someone over. Do some of the sorting and putting away you've been putting off. Paint a room. Go to the library for a good book. Try a new computer game. As the British say, "Carry on."

CHAPTER 15

Helping Yourself

ACCORDING TO A 1987 SURVEY by Runzheimer International, 71 percent of the employee relocations that fail (the employee returns to a job in the old location) fail because of the family's inability to adjust to the new location.

"That can't be right!" you say.

It is. But listen carefully. I didn't say 71 percent of relocations fail, I said 71 percent of the relocations *that* fail. Actually, only about 1 percent of all company-initiated relocations end with the return of the employee to his or her former location. And then the companies still help with the re-relocation costs, usually. Of course, this doesn't take into account those people who leave the job and return on their own or those who request transfer to yet another area. And no one's done a survey of people who relocate without employer support and "encouragement." So the figure is surely higher than 1 percent.

The number, however, is not the important factor in this bit of information. What is important is that almost three-quarters of the known reversals are prompted by family problems! Here we have a survey that confirms what everyone knows: moving is not easy on the person relocating for a new job *or* on the people who go along.

Some corporations are so aware of the stress generated by family adjustment problems that they have instituted programs to help. There are new employees' get-together groups that include spouses and children. Professional counseling group sessions are sometimes made available. Occasionally, companies even offer complimentary membership in country clubs or health clubs. But at the bottom line, relocation success still comes down to helping yourself. Let's look at some common stress symptoms in the home and see what you can do about them.

Overeating

There are only two kinds of people in this world: those who can't eat a thing under stress and those who eat so constantly that the opening and closing of the refrigerator door takes on a musical rhythm all its own. There seem to be a lot more of us in the refrigerator-oriented group than in the grit-your-teeth group, and weight gain is one of the hazards of relocation in America. Yes, food does seem to soothe the aching heart!

But is there anyone who wants to gain weight in this country? Hardly, I think. And giving in to the seemingly inevitable with "Oh, well, so I gain ten pounds or so. I can always take it off later" isn't a good solution. Besides the fact that virtually all medical authorities agree that gaining and losing (the yo-yo syndrome) is very bad for your body, those ten pounds get harder and harder to take off each time you have to lose them.

Some people fight fat alone, others join groups. Strangely enough, new medical research is finding that those who work at the battle of the bulge with company are more successful. In fact, the *Harvard Medical School Health Letter* stated recently, "Dieting is generally a social activity in our culture. Dieters tend to hang out or compare notes with other dieters."

It seems that in working with eating habits, we do better by sharing our thoughts, temptations, and hints for success. In the course of that sharing, many friendships are forged. So I heartily recommend joining a group if food is your source of comfort when you're lonely, bored, anxious, or angry. There are several ways to find a group appropriate to your needs.

Of course, you're familiar with the profit-making groups advertised in newspapers nationwide. They offer various programs, including weekly or sometimes even daily meetings, weigh-ins, rap sessions, you-can-do-it lectures, exercise programs, and behavior modification instruction. But there are other groups as well. OA, for example.

"OA?" you say. "Never heard of them."

Well, surely you've heard of AA (Alcoholics Anonymous). OA is Overeaters Anonymous. It's a nonprofit (the meetings are free) group structured exactly like AA. There are no weigh-ins and there is no prescribed diet. You choose whatever eating program and rules are suitable to your particular problem, and then on a day-by-day, hour-by-hour commitment you stick to those rules. There are numbers to call and people who will help, even to the point of coming to your house to sit with you, if necessary, or taking you out for a ride.

And you may be surprised to discover that the meetings are not a crowd of heavies. You may be sitting next to a beautiful woman who could well be a fashion model and hear her say, "Hi, I'm Catherine and I'm a compulsive overeater."

This program is not for everyone, but if you are interested, you can attend meetings without commitment and with complete anonymity. Meetings are held in hospitals, YMCAs, town halls, church basements, wherever a public place can be utilized. You will find a phone number listed under "Overeaters Anonymous" in the White Pages of the telephone directories of most major cities.

Other, less formally organized groups arrange their meetings in private houses, through religious organizations, through community groups such as United Way or the local YMCA, and sometimes through informal groups organized from the workplace. Find one that you feel comfortable with. You'll discover that you share similar problems with many others, and destroying your sense of isolation, your feeling that you are the only one who ever acted this way, is a major step in fighting the urge to eat for emotional reasons.

Smoking and Alcohol

If either or both of these are among your particular demons, be aware that they'll take on extra powers during a relocation. When people are under stress or lonely or disoriented or uncertain, they reach for comfort. And sometimes comfort is a devil in disguise.

As in the problem of overeating, there are groups, both commercial and noncommercial, to assist you in combating these problems. Join one, if only for a short time. But be aware that you are not as likely to forge new friendships here as are the people in the eating-problem groups. Somehow the doing-it-together feeling is not as strong, except among the very supportive people of AA.

Perhaps the best advice I can give you for combating the urge for a cigarette or an extra drink is not to sit at home alone feeling sorry for yourself. Get out of the house and do something. Find a volunteer group, ride horses, take a moonlighting job, get involved in the parents' organization at your child's school.

Anxiety Attacks

An anxiety attack is a frightening experience that can have many physical manifestations. Some people get all of them, some only one or two. Among the most common are: sweaty palms, racing heart, dizziness, feelings of extreme fatigue, a sudden fear that you cannot accomplish a routine task, inability to leave the security of your home or workplace, and sudden fear of travel. Some people also pick at their nails or skin or pull out eyebrows, eyelashes, or even their hair.

Some people experience the symptoms of anxiety during the stressful period itself, while others experience them when the stress is over and everything should be just fine. The condition is more puzzling and frightening for the second of these two groups, since offers of support are less quick in coming. Friends and relatives keep asking, "What's the matter? Everything is all right now!" and often the person experiencing the poststress anxiety cannot answer.

Most people think of anxiety as an emotional problem, but you may be surprised to know that it is also a physiological process and that some individuals are biologically more prone to it than others. If you think you might be having anxiety attacks, do try to find a good medical doctor and explain your symptoms and your suspicions as to their cause to him or her. There are medications on the market that can alleviate your anxiety responses and help you through the stress periods.

I know what some of you are thinking. This is the age of overmedication and, perhaps even more, the age of the fear of overmedication. The "in" thing to do today is not "take anything," work through whatever your problem is with diet and exercise. But sometimes such self-prescribing only adds stress by beginning a vicious circle. A person tries a program and fails *because* of the stress he or she is under and then starts on the I-can't-do-it or I-didn't-try-hard-enough guilt trips. All of which adds to the stress and increases the anxiety.

If you need medical help, get it. Taking a medication for a few months under a doctor's supervision is not likely to get you hooked for life.

The Blues

There's a difference between an anxiety attack, a clinical depression, and "the blues." Many people feel down, don't know what to do with themselves, and just see life as meaningless for brief periods now and then, especially after the trauma of a move. Relocation research shows that spouses who do not work outside the home are most often affected by this problem. The most common folk solution is to get out and go shopping. Some women actually become shop-a-holics. After all, there is a house to be decorated, new furniture needed, new appliances, new clothes to suit the new climate, etc., etc., etc.

Be warned that there is danger in repeated shopping sprees immediately following a move. Many people buy inappropriately and find themselves sorry a few months later. It's really better if you can let yourself settle into your new home and new environment a bit before spending large amounts of money on furniture and decorating. This may mean living with someone else's cabbage roses on the walls until you get the feel of your new living space. But if you can wait out a short settling-in period, you will not be as likely to make decisions that are tied to trying to make this new space just like, or completely different from, your old home.

Psychologists and Psychiatrists

Finding one is hard. So much depends upon the mix of your personalities. Your best source of information is usually other people who personally know how the counselor works. But how do you find such people when you're new in town?

If your children or teens need help, try consulting with school guidance counselors. These people have seen success and failure with other students. They are most likely to know which counselors in the community are best suited to deal with a particular problem. Of course, you might also ask your pediatrician for some names. But, then again, you may not yet have found a pediatrician with whom you are satisfied!

For adults, ask your company relocation counselor or the company medical department if they have a file of recommended counselors. You might also ask your physician or call the local hospital for a list of recommended psychiatrists. Be aware, however, that first-rate academic training and achievements do not necessarily mean that a particular psychiatrist or psychologist will be right for you.

Start therapy on a try-out basis. After a session or two, you will have a feeling as to whether the interaction of your personality and your therapist's methods and attitudes will work or not. Don't be afraid to say to a psychologist, "I don't think this is going to work, because I don't feel comfortable with you," or "because you remind me of my father," or whatever other aspect of the relationship bothers you. Having been given this kind of information, the psychologist may even recommend someone else who can work more directly with your particular problem.

Self-Help Groups

In January of 1981, New Jersey became the first state in the nation to establish a statewide, computerized referral system for self-help groups. Since then, several other states have followed, and today there is a national clearinghouse for self-help groups: National Self-Help Clearinghouse, 33 West 42nd Street, New York, NY, 10036, (212) 840-1259.

This group will refer you to self-help regional clearinghouses and to self-help groups around the country. They publish a newsletter, run research projects, and provide technical assistance to individuals and groups.

A directory of self-help groups around the country, called *The Self-Help Source Book*, is available from: The New Jersey Self-Help Clearinghouse, 50 Morris Avenue, Denville, NJ, 07834, (201) 625-7101.

There are groups for almost everything, and if you can't find a group that seems to suit your particular problem, you can think about starting one. Information on how to do that is available from the National Self-Help Clearinghouse.

Should You Ever Say No to Relocation?

Transfers are refused and the people who refuse them do keep their jobs. People do decide not to relocate even though opportunity seems to beckon elsewhere. This is a decision you and your family must make, weighing risk against potential reward.

The study of the effects of relocation on individuals has attracted some very fine psychologists during the past decade. Today, there are even professional companies that specialize in psychological testing to predict how an employee will adapt to a relocation. How accurate these tests are remains to be seen.

Among the factors that should be considered as indicators of a possibly difficult relocation are:

- Never moved before.

- Especially close ties with family in the current community.

- A parent or older family member in the community who will not move with the relocating family but needs assistance or will probably need assistance in the near future.

- A spouse with a well-established career.

- Children in high school.

- A family member with an illness or disability that demands specialized care.

- Any particularly strong commitment to a religious, community, or social group.

Bear in mind that these factors should not automatically rule out a relocation. They just indicate that there will probably be some difficulty. Knowing this is the first step to overcoming the problem. Get facts and professional opinions. Then make your decision.

PART III

Things to Do

CHAPTER 16

Lightening the Load

WHEN THE COMPANY PAYS for everything, or when you're only moving to the next town and you can transport station wagon loads at a time, there's a temptation to save things. "Well, this is still good . . ." seems to prevail even though you may not have used that particular item a single time during the past three years. When you're paying for the move yourself, however, those three boxes of textbooks from your sophomore year at Upandcoming College are going to cost you both money and effort. (And by the time your son or daughter studies any subject in those boxes the material will be dated if not dead.)

Relocation is a good time to reconsider what you really need and use in your life and to unload some of the excess baggage you've been carrying around.

Sorting

Before you call in a moving company for an estimate, you should go through your home, room by room, and sort out what you want to take with you and what you want to get rid of. This will take some time. You'll have to go through the closets, the kitchen and bathroom cabinets, the attic, the basement, and the garage. Mark those things you do not plan to take so that you will be sure to point them out to the person doing the estimate for the moving company.

The Tag Sale

Tag sale, relocation sale, garage sale, moving sale, they all mean the same thing: a sale by a private party of used items. Prices are always at huge discounts off the retail value of the same items new. Such sales have become popular all over the country. Many real estate brokers even give out free signs that say GARAGE SALE with arrows so that you can mount them on street corners. And most sales are very successful. Even people who think they don't have much to sell are surprised at how much money they make at their tag sale.

In the Hands of the Pros

Tag sales have, in fact, become so popular that they have given birth to a business. In many parts of the country, you can hire tag sale professionals to run your sale. If you have antiques, paintings, or valuable collector's pieces, you may want to seek out these people. Or you may choose to hire a professional for other reasons. Some people just can't bear to watch the merchandising of their personal belongings. They come close to tears if no one wants the dusty-rose sofa that was once Grandma's or when low offers come in and price-haggling starts. They even get a lump in their throats as two-years-dead Rover's old doghouse is carted off. Other people simply do not feel secure in arranging, pricing, and holding the sale.

Tag sale professionals will usually take care of all advertising, sorting, pricing, and marketing of the goods you have for sale.

Sometimes they will call in professional appraisers for the price valuation of special items. They usually charge either a per-hour fee or a percentage of the profits. Twenty-five percent is pretty much the going rate, but anything can be negotiated.

It is a good idea to have a contract with your tag sale manager. This should be a written agreement that states what services will be performed and the commission or salary to be paid. The professional tag sale manager should also carry insurance against any damages to your home by customers or theft of particularly valuable goods. Ask about the insurance. And be certain that your own homeowner's policy will cover your liability if someone should trip and fall or otherwise get hurt on your premises during the sale or during the preparation work for it. If you want complete freedom from the job of disposing of your unwanteds, you should also ask if the tag sale manager will remove the goods that don't sell.

Running Your Own Sale

If you wish to run your own sale, most experts advise that you spend a little time going to some nearby sales, especially those run by professionals. At these sales, you will get some good ideas for displaying various types of merchandise and you will get a sense for the market value of various items.

Everyone agrees that tag sales move along better if the merchandise is organized and displayed by kind. For example, put all tableware together on a cloth-covered table, hang clothes on a rack (you can rent one at most rental companies), group housewares and small appliances on another table, gather sports equipment in one corner and children's toys in another.

Price tags should be the stick-on kind that are easily removable. These are available in most stationery stores and at Woolworth's throughout the country. Be sure everything is marked. Unmarked items do not sell as quickly, especially if your sale is crowded and getting a price quote means waiting to ask.

Advertise your sale in several local newspapers. If community bulletin board space is available in local supermarkets, post 8½-by-11 sheets of paper advertising your sale. Include clear directions to your property (many people won't come if they think it's too hard to find) and headline with a few lead items. Sports equipment, antiques, and children's clothes are good leaders.

If your town will allow it, post TAG SALE signs with an arrow pointing in the direction to be taken to your property at all the intersections near your home.

Allow two days for your sale. You can reduce items that aren't sold during the first day on the second. If the weather is terrible during the two days of your sale, hold it again the next weekend. Avoid holidays except Memorial Day, July Fourth when it comes on a weekend, and Labor Day. These dates seem to bring out more buyers.

Expect to bargain on the prices of larger items, usually giving yourself a 10 percent leeway. If you feel you don't want to come down on a particular item at the outset of the sale, tell the prospective buyer that you'll reduce the price the next day, but it might get sold before that.

Do not hold items without a substantial cash deposit, for which you should give a receipt with both the amount of deposit and the item to be purchased named. Many people will tell you they are just going home to get the cash and never return. Meanwhile the item is off the market during prime buying time.

Have a cashbox and remove most of the cash you collect at frequent intervals. Keep change and small bills handy, however. Do not let customers into your house unescorted, even to use the bathroom or the telephone. It's always a good idea to have at least two people, preferably three, running the sale.

Have plenty of brown paper grocery bags or plastic shopping bags ready and keep a pile of newspapers near your cashier for wrapping glass items. Of course, your cashier should also have a calculator. And be sure to put fresh batteries into it before the sale.

Whether or not you take personal checks is a decision you must make for yourself, perhaps on an individual basis for each customer. If you decide you will take checks, however, be sure to ask for identification.

Donations

No one sells everything at a tag sale. So what are you going to do with the stuff that's left over? If you decided you wanted to unload it once, it's probably not a good idea to decide to keep it after all. Before you call the Haulitaway Service, however, think about making donations.

Many religious groups accept used furniture and clothing to help needy families. Call one in your area and see what they will take for you. Several national charity organizations such as Goodwill and the Salvation Army will send a truck to your home to pick up donations.

If you have furniture among your leftovers, you might also try calling some local theater groups or even the theater director of your local high school. These groups always need furniture for their productions. Clothes, too, especially if you have some old period-type costumes.

Free Items

If there are some things you'd like out of your life immediately, have a FREE corner in your tag sale. You'll be surprised what people will cart away when it's marked TAKE ME, I'M YOURS. You might even mention that some free items are included when you compose your ad for the local newspapers. Such notification will bring some people out in a hurricane.

When It's Over

Don't forget to take down all the signs you put up or you may have people popping in the following weekend. Then turn back to your belongings and say to yourself, "Okay! All this is going with us!"

CHAPTER 17

Connections Here and There

IF YOUR MOVE takes you across state lines, you will truly begin
to understand the name of our country: the United *States* of
America. I think you'll be surprised at how much of your life is
controlled by local government. In fact, you'll have to take steps to
become a citizen of your new state in order to protect your rights.
Let's run through some of the points that are important.

Licenses

Every state has its own licensing procedures, requirements, restric-
tions, and time limitations. And just about everything in your life
that requires a license is state-controlled.

Driver's licenses affect more people than any other kind of
license. Most states allow several weeks of permanent residence
before the requirement to change a license, and sometimes licensing is reciprocal. You hand in your old license and your new state
issues another. In other states, you will be required to take a new
written examination on state and federal road laws. Get a booklet

from the motor vehicle department of your new state and study! Although you can usually retake these tests again and again until you pass, there is always a time delay and you don't want to be without a license. You may also be surprised at how much you have forgotten in the *x* number of years since you took a driving test. In a few states, you must not only take a written test, but also pass a road test and a vision examination. Find out what the requirements are before you move so that you can prepare yourself in advance.

Auto registrations are not, strictly speaking, a license, but you can't drive a car without one, so I will include them here. Most states require proof of insurance and title in order to register an automobile. This may cause some problem if your car is financed in your old location, since some finance companies will not issue the title to a car until the loan balance is paid in full. Check with your auto finance company about its policy. You may have to pay off the loan in one location and then refinance in the other. Or the loan company may supply satisfactory title information to the motor vehicle department.

Professional licenses and certifications can cause real delays in reestablishing your business or career, so try to make plans for licensing in your new state as far in advance as possible. Among the careers requiring licensing supervised by states are virtually all medical careers, dentists, veterinarians, pharmacists, teachers, real estate and insurance brokers and salespeople, financial advisers, accountants, lawyers, plumbers, heating and electrical contractors, hairdressers, certain types of engineers, architects, private detectives, psychologists in private practice, and, in some areas, builders.

To obtain information on the requirements for licensing in the state that you are going to, contact the state agency or commission that oversees the licensing procedure for your trade or profession. Or you can contact your national trade or professional organization. If licensing examinations must be taken, schedule as far in advance as possible, since there are long waits in some fields. In some cases, teachers for example, temporary certification or licensing may be available while the newly relocated person completes specific state education requirements.

Recreational licenses vary greatly from state to state. Gun permits may or may not be reciprocal, but hunting and fishing licenses must be obtained in each state. Some states also require licensing for snowmobiles and mopeds and special licenses for motorcycles. Be sure to check the laws in the new state before you take out your vehicle for its first run.

Domicile

Establishing your primary residence is important for tax and legal purposes. Unless you do so, you may find yourself paying state income tax in two states quite legally. And in some places there are other laws to complicate domicile. In Washington, D.C., for example, you cannot spend more than 183 days in your Washington residence without paying taxes as though you were a District of Columbia citizen. This is true even if you have firmly established your domicile in another state!

To establish domicile, some states issue a certificate of domicile. If yours does not, you can establish it by your voter registration. Property ownership and automobile registration help but do not establish domicile beyond legal question.

Of course you'll change your address at your old post office and arrange to have your mail forwarded. But don't count on this activity to establish domicile. You can have any number of postal addresses, but only one domicile. Speaking of the post office, remember that forwarding magazines costs big bucks. Even if you do not know your new permanent address when you leave your old home, notify the magazines to which you subscribe of your new whereabouts. If you don't have a street address, take out a post office box in your new area or have the mail sent general delivery and arrange with the new post office to hold it until you can pick it up at regular intervals.

Wills

State laws regarding wills differ, but even if you move to a state that will recognize a will written in another state, your heirs may have trouble with probate. The best advice is to have a new will written in the state you have moved to as soon as you can. The same goes for trusts.

Financial Matters

Many stockbrokers now have toll-free numbers, so it is possible to leave your stock accounts with your present broker. If you wish to change to a branch office nearer your home, have your broker do the paperwork and get to know your new salesperson as soon as possible. Transferring your accounts to another firm is more complicated and could involve selling some stocks you don't really want to sell at the moment. But, of course, it can be done.

Insurance on your house and car should be handled locally. Some insurance companies have representatives nationwide, others are limited to working within one state. Ask your present insurance agent to find out whether the company that currently writes your insurance operates in the area you are going to. Your life insurance policies can either be left with the main office or transferred to a regional office nearer to your residence. Be sure to notify them of your change of address.

Checking accounts can cause problems in some parts of the country where banks require that money be on deposit for up to two weeks before it can be withdrawn. Some people establish checking accounts while they are on their house-hunting trips, ordering checks with their names imprinted but no address.

If you must open your checking account *after* you arrive in your new location, you may be able to have the bank waive its waiting period by using traveler's checks for your initial deposit. Don't count on a cashier's check giving you immediate access to your money, however, since some banks require a waiting period even on these. The most important advice of all is: don't close your old account before you open and establish your new one. After you are functioning with your new bank, you can have your old bank send you a cashier's check for your balance or you can have it wired directly to your new bank.

Certificates of deposit are another matter. Often you cannot withdraw or move these funds until they mature without incurring substantial penalties. Meet with someone in the bank before you leave and sign any papers necessary to have your money sent to your new location as soon as your certificates mature.

Credit cards have become a national game. Even if you live in New York City, you might carry a Visa card or a MasterCard from a bank in New Mexico. There is usually no need to change the bank that issues your credit cards, only your address. Unless, of course, you discover that there are better rates and terms in your new location.

One of the problems I have encountered in closing credit card accounts is the interest charge. Even if you pay the total balance due on the day you receive the statement in the mail, you will most likely get another statement the following month saying that you have 57 cents, or some other ridiculous figure, still due. This is, of course, *interest*, since you didn't pay the balance in full at the time the computer was printing out your statement. To avoid hassle, I usually overpay my bill by a bit more than the interest that was charged for the present month. If you do this, you will get a statement saying you have a credit balance the following month. Then you can call the credit card company and tell them to send you a check for the credit balance. Once you have the check in hand and a zero balance in your account, notify the credit card company in writing that you wish to close your account.

Long-distance real estate ownership can be a problem or a lovely source of income. If you own rental property or a vacation home in your old location, you might choose to sell it and reinvest in your new location, where you can supervise personally. But if property in your old area is appreciating faster than property in your new area, you may want to hold on to your investments. In that case, my best advice is to hire a reliable property management firm. Rental property tends to slide downhill without occasional visits from the owner or a representative.

By holding vacation property, you may be able to keep in touch with an area that you love. Again, however, it is important to hire a trustworthy person to oversee your property. You may or may not use a real estate agent to handle your rentals, but you need someone else to see to the plumbing, electricity, storm damage, yard work, and general upkeep of the place.

Sometimes people forget that their household goods are also a financial asset. It is important to take an inventory of all you own even before the moving company appraiser arrives at your home. List the items by room, include approximate value, identifying features, condition, age, etc. Many movers advise that you also take pictures of anything of particular value so that you can substantiate the item and its condition.

Medical Matters

Finding new doctors, dentists, veterinarians, etc., in a new area is one of the prime concerns of relocation. One method is to ask your current medical practitioner for a referral to someone in your new area. If he or she does know someone, you may be in luck. But be aware that many physicians have closed practices that are limited to the number of patients that they can handle. Even a referral from another physician may not get you into a closed practice.

Of course, one of the oldest ways to find a doctor is to ask your new acquaintances for the names of the professionals they are using. This works sometimes, but sometimes what's right for your neighbor may not be right for you. So be prepared to change, if necessary.

Because finding a doctor, especially the right specialist, is an increasingly difficult problem, some of our largest hospitals, such as Mount Sinai in New York City, have medical referral systems. If you call the hospital's referral number and describe your symptoms, they will give you several names of physicians in that specialty who are associated with the hospital.

You have a right to your medical and dental records. If you are not sure what doctor and dentist you will be using in your new area, you can ask that these be given to you. Some people, however, prefer to find their new physicians first and then arrange to have medical records sent directly to his or her office. If you have special conditions in which X ray or other imaging records are vital to treatment or future diagnosis, get copies of these and take them with you. Perhaps the most common carry-along is the baseline mammogram.

Finding a good veterinarian is almost harder than finding a good doctor, for your pet cannot tell you how well it has been treated. Before you start your search, however, be sure that you have obtained your pet's inoculation and medical records from your current veterinarian. You will need them if you must board your pet, and you will need evidence of rabies vaccination to license your dog in most states.

I have found that the best tactic in the hunt for a good veterinarian is calling several dog breeders in the area and asking them which veterinary hospital they use and how satisfied they are. I suggest dog breeders because their names are the easiest to get. You can call the American Kennel Club in New York City and they will send you a list of breeders in your area, or you can just look in the local newspaper classified section under "Pets." There you will find any number of people trying to sell their purebred puppies. It has been my experience that dog breeders are usually most willing to help a new person in the area, even if you are not interested in buying a puppy. This is an especially good tactic if you call someone selling puppies in a breed that you also own, for they can give you information on local dog organizations that may help you to make connections in your new area.

But what if you're looking for a veterinarian for your cat, horse, or parrot? Well, you might see some of those advertised in the paper, too. If not, try the dog people. Few will be too busy to talk with you for a bit about their veterinarians.

Education

School records are also yours for the asking. Some people wait until their children are registered in their new school, give that school the name and address of the old school, and let the school staff do the work. I suggest that you do *not* do this. Records can be long in coming, and in the interim your child can be assigned to the wrong classes. Take the records with you and present them when you register your child in his or her new school.

Special References

As I mentioned in the "Feelings" section, one of the problems of moving children is their loss of a sense of identity. They must start all over again to prove how good they are in sports, or cheerleading, or drama, or music. And sometimes very fine talent gets lost in sheer numbers.

I strongly recommend that you get reference letters for your children that relate to the after-school activities in which they will probably participate. Some activities, like Red Cross swimming ranks, or ranks in various kinds of karate, or scouting achievements, are supported by national organizations. Be sure your child has an up-to-date certificate from these organizations so that he or she will be placed properly.

For nonranked activities, such as sports, drama, art, or music, have the current coach, leader, or teacher write an evaluation so that, for example, the new music teacher will know that John can play three of the Chopin études. The evaluation should also include what has been done or studied and what plans the teacher had had for future study.

There is also some loss of identity for adults in a move. Most groups will take you at your word that you were treasurer of the garden club, but how about your volunteer work in the hospital for severely disabled children? You may not have earned any money, but your skills may be those of a highly trained professional. A letter from the supervisor of the hospital outlining your duties and the kind of work you have been doing may get you a similar position near your new residence without the hassle of trial periods or menial jobs to fill the time until you prove yourself. This advice holds true for many kinds of special interest groups—a historical society, for example, or a friends of the library board, or a counseling or hot line center run by a local religious group. The letter is not a ticket in, it is an introduction and an evaluation of the skills you possess. It can be as important as your driver's license in some identification situations.

VIT (Very Important Trivia)

Don't forget to cancel, get final readings on, and pay the final bills of:

Your electric company,
Your water company,
Your gas company or your oil delivery service,
Your sewer use bill,
Your condominium maintenance fees,
Your recreational association dues,
Your home newspaper delivery,
Your telephone bill (local and long-distance).

And don't forget to arrange for new connections in your new location.

CHAPTER 18

About Moving Men

THEY'RE HUMAN, you know. They come to work after a sleepless night with a sick baby. They work with a headache or a cold. They get tired and hungry. And sometimes they get mad.

These are the people who will carry your leather sofa and the boxes that hold your great-grandmother's china. Be nice to them. The attitude of the person whose goods are being transported can have a tremendous effect upon the condition and delivery of those goods.

I don't mean that you should be fawning or intimidated (even though a 250-pound moving man can be intimidating) but that you should treat these men who are working for you as you might like to be treated if you were working for them. Respect their expertise and their efforts, anticipate some of their needs, be there but don't be bothersome.

According to a group of moving men I interviewed, the worst thing a relocating person can do is try to help with the furniture. Moving men have been trained in how to lift and maneuver heavy and bulky items. They have learned to work as a team and to rely on each other. When the shipper (that's you) gets involved in trying to help lift or steer, everyone tenses up and accidents tend to happen. Let the men do the work their way; just be there to answer questions.

A supply of ice water in summer, or coffee in winter, is a kindness most moving men appreciate. A box of doughnuts at coffee-break time might bring about extra special care.

Every moving man that I interviewed told me that it is important for an adult family member to be in the house during packing and loading. Not only do questions inevitably come up, but also a bill of lading must be filled out during this time. It will list all your possessions and the condition they are in. When complete, it will be given to you and you will be asked to sign it. Read it over carefully. Be sure that you agree with the condition noted for each item.

Once you sign it, you will be given a copy of the bill of lading. Keep it in a safe and convenient place, since you will be asked to go over it again in your new location to verify that everything was delivered. Do not feel pressured, however, to check out the top, bottom, back, and sides of every piece of furniture as it comes in the door. In most cases, you have ninety days to report damages to your property and file an insurance claim.

Believe it or not, it's even more important that you be in your new residence while your goods are being unloaded. Movers tell me that the single consideration they most appreciate is someone at the door of the new residence who will tell them exactly where each piece of furniture or box should go. There is nothing so frustrating as standing in a foyer holding a fully loaded dresser while a husband and wife argue about which room it should go into.

In order to direct your movers most effectively, you should spend some time beforehand planning what goes into each of the new rooms. You can do this with graph paper, drawing each room to scale, or you can buy furniture-arranging kits of graph paper and stick-on furniture pieces from stationery stores and from many of the major moving companies. If you have a floor plan of your new residence ready with furniture laid out, you can direct the moving men exactly where to put your pieces.

The person by the door should not leave for any extended period of time without a substitute. Movers are driven crazy by the family that says, "We're just going out to lunch. Be back in twenty minutes," and then returns two hours later. Remember, an awful lot of where-does-this-go furniture and boxes can be stacked in the living room in two hours!

At one time (as recently as 1980) paying a mover meant paying cash or its equivalent in a certified check. While either of these two methods is still acceptable, more and more movers are accepting credit cards for payment, and some moving companies even arrange their own credit accounts. Be certain to find out how your mover wants to be paid before you sign a contract.

Then there's the question of tips. Does anyone know what's right? How hard have your men worked? Was there a steep driveway involved? Did the thermometer outside the kitchen window reach 98 degrees? Or maybe 10 below? Was it raining? Did you have a particularly large load of strange and valuable pieces? Only you can determine the appropriate tips. Consider, however, that you might tip a waiter $10 for perhaps two hours' service and a bellhop $2 for carrying two suitcases to your hotel room using an elevator to bypass the stairs.

Guarantees

Moving household goods is the business of juggling trucks, manpower, schedules, and destinations, and sometimes working around the weather. Essentially, there are no guarantees. But if you must have your household goods picked up and delivered on specific dates, you can pay for a guaranteed pickup or delivery date. This still does not guarantee your date, but it does mean that the mover will pay a fine, usually $125 a day plus living costs, if he does not perform as specified in the contract.

To help guarantee your guarantees, try to schedule moves in the middle of the month, when there is less demand. Also be certain that the driver has your correct address in the new location. Be aware that if yours is a new house in a new development of houses, its street may not be on currently published street maps. If you even think this might be the case, machine-copy a street map that you have and then draw in the new street and mark the location of your house. If you are moving to a large garden-type condominium complex, hand-draw a map of the buildings, indicate their names or numbers, and mark the exact location of your apartment. Also be sure to give your driver a phone number where you can be reached during the days between pickup and delivery.

Insurance

There are a number of different kinds of liability insurance available since the deregulation of the industry in 1980. And your homeowner's policy may or may not cover your goods while in transit. Check with your insurance agent.

If you wish to buy insurance from your mover, ask to see the various offerings and choose among them to get the coverage that is right for you. If you have something particularly valuable, let's say a 1919 Steinway grand piano, you might want to take out special insurance on that piece through your homeowner's company rather than the moving company. Computers also are susceptible to damage during a move, and you might want to check with the manufacturer for special packing instructions as well as take out special item insurance. It is important that you tell the moving company estimator that you have several things that need special packing when he or she is doing the estimate. Materials for making custom crates will then be sent on the day the moving men come to do the packing.

What do you do if there is a problem with your insurance coverage and you dispute the company's decision? Well, before you sign up, check to see if your mover is a member of the American Arbitration Association. If so, you can have your complaint settled by an arbiter who renders a legally binding decision. This will usually take much less time and much less money than going to court to settle a difference.

Doing Your Own Packing

Start with the things that are out of season or that you won't be using in the interim, your fine china and silver, for example, unless you expect to entertain before your move. Use small boxes. You'd be surprised at how heavy even a modest-sized box can be.

If you can't get the boxes you need from your local liquor store or grocery store, you can buy boxes from your truck rental company or from local movers. The boxes will be delivered flat, however, and you will have to assemble them. Be sure to have a good supply of strapping tape available to secure the bottoms. You don't want to face the nightmare of packing a box, picking it up, and having its contents fall out the bottom as you walk.

Special wardrobe cartons for your clothes are also available from the local movers and worth the money. You should order one for each closet in your home. You can then remove all the garments on their hangers, hang them in the wardrobe carton, and simply rehang them in the closets when you get to your destination.

Try to pack one room at a time, keeping all the items for that room in boxes marked as such. If you mix things from different rooms in the same box, your unpacking will take longer. Be sure to have an adequate supply of strapping tape, labels, and marking pens available. Write the contents of each box and its destination on the outside. Or you might number the boxes and keep your inventory on cards matched to each box by number. If you use this number/card method, do not omit marking the room destination on the top of the box. Whenever appropriate, mark FRAGILE, BREAKABLE, or CRUSHABLE clearly on the top and sides. You can buy THIS SIDE UP stickers at most stationery stores.

The day before moving day, secure all appliances. You can buy tub locks at your local hardware store for washer and dryer tubs. After securing these in place, you can pack them full of soft items such as your pillows and quilts or your child's stuffed-animal collection.

Wrap dishes in newspaper or bubble wrap. You can buy bubble wrap from moving companies. If you are wrapping anything that might stain permanently, however, wrap it first in plastic garbage bags, then in newspaper, because newspaper print comes off in a black blur. If you prefer, you can buy white wrapping paper from movers or moving supply houses. Sometimes all these items are also available from your truck rental center.

Mirrors, glass tabletops, and paintings need special crates. If you are using a moving company for loading and transport, I suggest that you leave these items for professional packing. Tell the company representative exactly what will be left for the movers to crate and provide the company with exact measurements of each item so that materials for appropriate crates will be available on the day of the move.

Pets, Paints, Plants, and Other No-Nos

There are some things that the Interstate Commerce Commission will not allow your mover to move. Among them are all flammable materials. That means paints are out. Also all turpentine, oil, cleaning solvents, and gasoline. You will have to empty your lawn mower, your snowblower, and even your gasoline-driven chain saw.

Plants can be difficult. Most wouldn't survive the packing process even if the mover could carry them. Make a gift of your prize beauties to friends or nursing homes and start afresh in your new location.

No pets of any kind can go in the moving van. Dogs and cats can be put in specially designed air cargo crates and flown to the destination city on all the major airlines. Horse transportation must be arranged in special animal vans. Tropical fish are perhaps best given to friends. Birds are a problem because some states will not allow them across state lines (especially parrots).

Unpacking

How much unpacking you want the moving men to do is up to you, guided perhaps by your budget. Most movers will put your beds back together and place your furniture where you tell them. If you wish all the boxes unpacked, you had better have very definite plans as to where you want everything to go. Sometimes it's easier to leave some things in their boxes until you decide where you will want them later. You must also decide on what you want the movers to remove. In some areas of the country, there are dump site shortages and you cannot put large cardboard cartons at the curb except at specified times of the year. If you don't want to live with those boxes, folded or not, arrange to have the movers take them away.

When You Do It Yourself

This is no picnic, folks. Moving is tough work and a misjudgment can cost you money in lost or damaged goods, or worse, an injury to a member of your moving crew. But do-it-yourself moving does save money. It is most frequently successful for short moves and/or moves of a relatively small amount of goods.

Having chosen your best deal from a truck rental firm, you will have to decide what size truck you will need. Most rental companies have brochures available describing the trucks and the types of furnishings and goods they will hold. Make a list of all your belongings and try to pick the van and contents description that comes closest to matching your list.

Be aware that you can rent dollies and many packing supplies from the truck rental company. Among the available items are padded straps, ropes, and padded furniture covers. You can also rent car-top carriers and tow bars.

Be sure to reserve your truck at least several weeks in advance. Longer, if you are moving during the peak season (May to September) or if you are moving during the busiest days (the end and beginning of each month). And let me remind you again to check your insurance coverage. Some homeowner's policies will allow you to buy riders that will insure your goods while they are in transit even if *you* are doing the transporting. This is an investment in peace of mind well worth its cost.

When you begin loading the van, load the heavy appliances first, right behind the cab. Tie mattresses on their edges to the sides of the van so that they will not shift or buckle. Against the mattresses tie mirrors and large pieces of glass in the special crates you have made for them. Load large pieces of furniture next, using pads to protect each piece. Fill in spaces with small boxes. Whenever possible remove table legs, tape the bolts to the bottom of the table, and pack it on its side in the van. Use padded straps or ropes around dressers and china cabinets so that doors or drawers do not open.

The secret of least damage is a tightly packed van. Fill the space from bottom to top using cushions, pads, small boxes, and small pieces of furniture as spacers. Rugs should be rolled and packed in the middle of the van. What you are putting together here is a three-dimensional jigsaw puzzle. And you want it to come out with as few empty spaces as possible.

Unless you are an experienced truck driver, be aware that when you close the doors on the van and climb inside the cab, you are embarking on a new experience. Oh, most of the newer trucks do have automatic transmission, power steering, and a host of amenities found in plush cars, but the body of the vehicle you are driving is wider than the car you are accustomed to, and it is also longer. You will have to allow more time in passing and much care. But then again maybe you won't be doing much passing.

The best advice for safety in doing a do-it-yourself move is: DRIVE SLOWLY. Allow plenty of space, more than you think you need, between you and the vehicle in front of you so that your braking can be slow and steady. Sudden braking can compress your cargo against itself, and those are *your* things that you might hear rattling around! Take corners and turns very slowly, so your household goods do not shift and bang side to side against each other.

And stop to rest. Moving is a big job. When you have finished packing, you're tired. Don't try to drive five hundred miles on the same day. Stop for meals and breaks, and if a responsible adult companion is available, take turns driving the van. You will function more efficiently and your household goods will be safer. Not to mention the safety of you yourself!

CHAPTER 19

Mastering the New Turf

WE SPENT ONE NIGHT in a house we had closed on that very afternoon. The moving van had not yet arrived and we each slept on the floor in the rooms that would become our bedrooms. Except that I didn't sleep much. The place was not only *not* home, it was damn scary. Besides every start of the furnace sounding as though the basement was about to blow up (to me, anyway) and every flush of a toilet sounding as though Niagara Falls had been transported to the space between the wallboards, there was that mental hospital two blocks away. I had known about this state facility when we bought the property, but its existence didn't bother me then. Now, in the dark on the floor, I imagined the mentally disturbed escaping and roaming round the windows of our "new home"!

Things got somewhat better after the furniture arrived. The awful echo subsided a bit. I hung curtains, even though they didn't match the walls, and the empty spaces began to fill up with the usual clutter. Neighbors introduced themselves, and I, of course, got over my fantasy of Peeping Toms in the night.

But there's an important message in this story. It's about sound. Unfamiliar sound is unsettling and echoes connote cold, empty, and uninhabited space. Home should be quiet and warm, or noisy and warm, but not echoing.

When you move into your new living space, put things up on the walls. They need not be permanent. And drape the windows for your privacy and for the softening effect on echoing sound in the house. Set up your stereo and your TV. Fill your new home with human sounds that are familiar and welcoming.

Finding the Way

Once you and your belongings have been deposited and temporarily arranged in your new living space, your immediate concern will be getting oriented. Most real estate agents and relocation consultants give out excellent street maps. Get at least three. Keep one in each of your cars. Then take another and tack it to a wall—the kitchen is probably the best choice.

This kitchen map will help you to get to know your community quickly, for you will use it to mark every spot that is important to you and your family. You can get as creative as you wish in doing this. Let the kids help. Use colored paper buildings or use pins with colored heads and name tag streamers.

First mark your living place on the map. Then begin the process of creating your mental map of the new area by marking the two-dimensional map. Every time you locate something, whether it be a supermarket, a pharmacy, the hospital, your children's schools, your workplaces, or a new friend's house, mark it on the map.

During the coming six months or so, the whole family will use this map to plan their comings and goings and to track where other family members are. Teens do especially well with this tactic. Since they know everything without being told, it is sometimes difficult to give them directions. It's much better to let the neutral map stand in for your admonishing voice.

My own fourteen-year-old son went out for a bike ride on the second day of one of our moves and didn't come home for six hours. Yes, he was lost. But would he admit it? Would he call home and ask for help? Not on your life! It was after this incident that our family devised the kitchen wall map as a safety net for everyone.

Have your teens mark the locations on the map of their friends' houses and the meeting places for groups in which they participate or the sports fields they use. Then whoever gets the job of pickup on a particular night will know, or be able to find out, where Juniper Field or the First Methodist Church Hall is.

For younger children, the kitchen map can be an asset in getting a sense of where they are in town if you help them to translate the information on the map to a visual sense of their movements. Remember, young children do not have highly developed map-reading skills. They will need personal guidance through the areas that they will be expected to know.

If your child walks to school or to the school-bus stop, don't just show him or her the map the first day or two. Walk the distance with your child, even if you must listen to "Aw, come on, Ma!" Point out particular landmarks on the route that will keep the child from getting lost.

If your children are invited to play at the houses of other children in the neighborhood, try to resist the temptation to drop them off on the way to do your grocery shopping. Children do not get a sense of direction when they travel in a car. If the distance is not too great, walk it with them, pointing out the turns and landmarks. On a second invitation, walk the route with them again, allowing them to tell you where to turn and why.

When you drive grade school children to school or to a Scout meeting, first trace the route on the wall map. Then as you drive, point out the turns. Children this age may never need to navigate this distance alone, but knowing the way to and from their frequent destinations will give them a sense of security. Also point out the routes to shopping centers, the hospital, and nearby police and fire stations. Then on another day when the children are in the car, have them tell you how to get to a named destination. If you do this carefully and your children ever do get lost or in trouble, they will have a sense of where they are in relationship to help.

Think of your kitchen wall map as a security blanket. It will make you feel better. You and the members of your family will be able to see on the wall your spot of belonging in the community and its relationship to the friends you have made and the facilities of the town. Be sure you mark the houses of adult friends in the neighborhood also so that you can show children where you might be or where they can go just in case you are not at home when they get there.

When you are first starting to get around town, identify major landmarks. Counting traffic lights is one way to keep your bearings, but it's much better to have something easily recognizable to indicate a turn (you can lose count of traffic lights). One friend always missed the left-hand turn to her street until her husband pointed out that there was a fence on the right-hand side of the road that looked just like the fences of Kentucky horse farms. At the end of the fence, there were exactly one hundred yards to the left-hand turn she had to take. Everyone in the family now uses the Kentucky horse farm fence as a marker.

Telephone Numbers

In the confusion of unpacking and settling in, it's easy to forget this chore. Don't! Look up and gather all the important local phone numbers soon after you move in. Your list should include fire, police, ambulance, hospital poison center, the workplaces of the adults, the schools your children attend, and the numbers of anyone you know in the community. Make copies of this list and post one near each of the extension phones.

Hang on to Old Habits

Paradoxically, one of the best ways to adjust to your new habitat is to hang on to some of the behavior patterns of your old. If you went out for pizza every Friday night in Goodville, go out for pizza in

Newtown. It may take you a few trips to find your dream place, but you will. One almost as good, or maybe even better, than your favorite at home. In doing this, you'll be establishing the ties that are necessary to change the new place into your hometown.

Chinese take-out restaurants can be found practically everywhere in the country. If you find one in your new town, try it out on a night when you're tired and the prospect of cooking dinner is dismal indeed. If the menu has some unknowns on it, try one each time you go. You may even find something you like better than the old standbys you ordered at home.

Discovering the restaurants of a new area is exciting. Search through newspaper advertisements and the Yellow Pages or follow the advice of new acquaintances. You'll get the opportunity to sample both regional and ethnic cooking (unless you limit yourself to McDonald's and Burger King).

If you are in the habit of going to the movies once a weekend, don't give that up either. Find out where the closest movie theaters are and mark them on your map. The same films that were showing in your old hometown will probably be available in your new, and your moviegoing will give you a sense of continuity. You're still part of the good old US of A!

Subscribe to the local papers as soon as you move in. This will help you to know what's going on, where to find things, who's having a sale, and what is of concern to the local citizens. And get library cards. Libraries have more than books nowadays. They are sources of multimedia entertainment and information, and some are actually becoming community centers.

Groups

If you were part of a religious group in your old town, take steps to find a group you will feel comfortable with in your new town. And don't be upset if the closest place of worship just doesn't seem right to you. Religious congregations, just like municipalities, have personalities. Attend services at several different locations until you find one where you feel comfortable. Religious groups and the social and community service functions that they sponsor are a good way to break into a new area and meet people who welcome you as one of their own.

If you were involved in civic groups (teacher aids, garden clubs, Meals-on-Wheels, whatever) in your old hometown, try to reestablish these habits in your new one. Also encourage your children to do the same. Scouts, 4-H, some programs like Tae Kwon Do self-defense training and Red Cross swimming programs are nationwide. Your new community will welcome your child at the same level that he or she had attained in the old hometown. This will help your child to regain identity and status in the new community.

Exercise

Perhaps most important of all, try to exercise regularly. I know this sounds like the boring "good health" advice you read in every magazine you pick up lately. But moving is a time of stress, and exercise does help to cut down the physiological effects of stress.

Walking is one of the best exercises going. And who knows? It may even help you to meet other walkers who are your neighbors. If walking is not convenient where you live, think about joining a health club or the local YMCA. Again, you will be doing your body a favor and you will be helping the feeling side of you make some new connections by meeting new people.

Many of you are probably thinking, "Oh, I'm just too busy to exercise. I can't spare the time. Look at the unpacking and decorating I have to do! That's surely enough exercise." Well, it isn't. The kind of exercise you need for stress release is sustained aerobic movement. Unpacking does not provide that. It also does not get you out of the house.

Try Out Some New Things

Every town, village, hamlet, city, even neighborhood offers something that is unique unto itself. A major part of your orientation
will be the discovery of these things in your new area. It may be a
flea market, a fabulous shopping mall, a local passion for a sport
you hardly knew existed, a tourist attraction within a few miles'
ride, or some bit of history. The library in the town next to us has a
ghost. Honestly. The lights in the stacks are kept lit all night and
most of the natives will tell you they've seen her shadow at some
time or another. Finding out the story of this innkeeper's daughter
(the library was a Revolutionary War inn before it was a library) who
opened a casket being stored for transportation in the back room of
the inn, looked upon her fiancé's body, and fell dead on the spot
was an interesting part of getting to know this area.

When you collect all the brochures that the real estate agents,
the relocation people, the banks, the Welcome Wagon lady, and the
insurance salespeople give you, don't just pile them on the dining
room table and leave them to gather dust. Within this printed
matter is information you'll want to know about the points of
interest and activities of the area. Investigate. You may be surprised
at what you discover not only about the area but also about yourself. The worst thing you can do when you relocate is stay home
and carefully unpack and place every item that you brought with
you. Go out. Look around. Let yourself grow!

Some Names and Numbers You Might Need

American Movers Conference
2200 Mill Road
Alexandria, VA, 22314
(703) 838-1930

Catalyst
(a not-for-profit organization that addresses topics related to the career
  advancement of women)
250 Park Avenue South
New York, NY, 10003
(212) 777-8900

Displaced Homemakers Network
1411 K Street N.W.
Room 930
Washington, D.C., 20005
(202) 628-6767

Employee Relocation Council
1720 N Street, N.W.
Washington, D.C., 20036
(202) 857-0857

Household Goods Carriers' Bureau
1611 Duke Street
Alexandria, VA, 22314
(703) 683-7410

Independent Relocation Consultants Association
2851 South Parker Road
Suite 900
Aurora, CO, 80014
(800) 235-5585

Insurance Information Institute
110 William Street
New York, NY, 10038
(212) 669-9200

National Self-Help Clearing House
33 West 42nd Street
New York, NY, 10036
(212) 840-1259

SchoolMatch
Public Priority Systems, Inc.
Blendonview Office Park
5027 Pine Creek Drive
Westerville, OH, 43801
(614) 890-1573

Index

ABOUT THE AUTHOR

Carolyn Janik has been a real estate professional for twenty years, both as an agent and as an advice columnist for *New Shelter Magazine*. She is most recently the author of *Money-Making Real Estate* and *All America's Real Estate Book* (with Ruth Rejnis). She lives with her family in New Jersey.